# SUCC[illegible] FROM WITHIN

Life-Changing Techniques,
Strategies and Insights That Unleash
Your Full Potential.

**Chris Hopkins**

Published by

MELROSE BOOKS

An Imprint of Melrose Press Limited
St Thomas Place, Ely
Cambridgeshire
CB7 4GG, UK
www.melrosebooks.co.uk

**FIRST EDITION**



Cover designed by Jeremy Kay

**ISBN 978-1-908645-83-8**



Printed and bound in Great Britain by:
CPI Group (UK) Ltd, Croydon, CR0 4YY

FSC
www.fsc.org
MIX
Paper from responsible sources
FSC® C013604

**This book is dedicated**
**to my lovely wife Mo.**

My life is filled with ups and downs. But whenever I have a bad day, I know I can always rely on you to support me and help me get through it. You are a constant source of strength and stability.

# CONTENTS

# FOREWORD

Many of us have experienced times in our life when we wish we could wave a magic wand and change our circumstances, make everything better. Start all over again; live a different life. Turn back the clock and do things differently. Success Starts From Within shows you how to tap into your extraordinary inner power and attract into your life all things you need to improve your situation. It reveals incredibly powerful ways to break free from destructive and harmful habits and take full control of your thinking. It teaches you how to think so positively and productively that you will feel yourself capable of achieving anything. What is this inner power? It is unshakeable belief. Continually thinking, talking and acting in a positive manner, as if you were already the person you would like to be, enjoying the life that you want and deserve.

This book is the result of over eighteen years of extensive research. The knowledge I've gained has provided me with the answers to many of life's big questions. Questions like: Why is one person happy and optimistic while another is forlorn and downbeat? Why is one person rich and successful while another is poverty-stricken and dispirited? Why is one person nervous and jittery and another self-assured and carefree? Why is one person happily married while another has a string of broken relationships? These and other questions are answered in Success Starts From Within. It was questions like these that drove me to research and write this book, and ultimately discover a new way of looking at how to fulfil your greatest desires.

We all want the best. None of us, though, want to end up disappointed. That's why we aspire no further than the best we think we're capable of attaining. We put any other thoughts to the back of our mind. We persuade ourselves that, even if we achieved greater success, we wouldn't really enjoy it. That's a shrewd self-protection mechanism, but it has one fundamental flaw. It means that when an opportunity arises to accomplish more, we tend to disregard it.

With Success Starts From Within you'll learn how to draw on knowledge, skills and expertise you didn't even know you possessed and how a few simple principles can free you from heartache, disappointment, anxiety, doubt and despair. Once you have incorporated these techniques into your daily routine, you will know how to face up to life's challenges, eliminate your fears and release your full potential. You'll find it illuminating, uplifting and inspiring.

All of us can develop unfaltering belief; it's simply a case of knowing how. Learning to think positively and creatively can open doors to unimaginable opportunities. It helps to unlock your potential and bring forth the genius that is lying dormant within you. You can become the unique person that it is in you to become, but only if you eradicate the negative thoughts that are holding you back. I show you how to think so positively and constructively that you'll believe you can achieve any goal you set for yourself. You will feel self-assured and courageous, and you will know that you have the potential to achieve more than you ever dreamed possible: and whatever you've achieved up until now is nothing compared to what you'll achieve from now on.

This book provides compelling proof that our beliefs about ourselves and the world around us alter our perception, our memory, our expectations, our energy, our health, our mood, our actions, our relationships, and eventually even our outward experiences. Throughout history, wise, enlightened and far-sighted people have held the basic understanding that what we believe we will somehow create. This book explores the mechanisms behind this amazing process, and shows you how to use these same techniques to create the most fulfilling beliefs we can.

Positive thinking is one of the most valuable tools in the world today for the enrichment of lives. It enables you to break undesirable habits, create desirable habits and constructively deal with and resolve every sort of human problem. We know that people who don't believe in themselves tend to fail, while those with self-belief will usually succeed. In Success Starts From Within, I explore the psychology behind how we create our own realities, and, more importantly, how we can change them for the better.

This inspiring book takes readers on a journey of self-discovery, redefining our understanding of ourselves and revealing the incredible inner resources we have at our disposal. You are taught how to achieve new and better results by employing simple, yet remarkably effective concepts and ideas for improving your situation. Anybody, regardless of their age or circumstances will benefit from adopting some of these innovative techniques that will help them ultimately accomplish any goal they set themselves. These are the same concepts used by high-achievers in every field. The processes, techniques and strategies I outline may seem simple, but do not be deceived. They are incredibly effective. Anyone who uses them will significantly increase their ability to make dramatic, life-enhancing differences. They show you how to unlock your true potential and bring forth the genius that is lying dormant within you. It will change your life.

# INTRODUCTION

Do you feel you can't move in any direction you choose? Are there times when you deeply desire to improve your situation, but think you lack the talent, intelligence and competence to achieve anything worthwhile? Could it be that what's holding you back is something far more constraining than any physical barrier? The likelihood is, you have a mental block. An irrational fear of being unworthy or incapable of pursuing certain options. Rise above these feelings of inadequacy by deciding what you want to be free of; and what you want to free yourself for. Start feeling that you're really moving forward and that you're going to overcome old obstacles, reach out to new challenges and alter lifelong habits. If you've been thinking for a long while about a plan or a possibility, go for it! It could change everything for the better.

For many years I was stuck in a dreary nine-to-five job, doing the same tedious routine day after day. No matter how hard I tried, I couldn't foresee myself ever getting out of this rut. The future looked bleak. As far as I was concerned, the odds were stacked against me. Success, fame and power were realistic goals for highly educated, intellectual people, or those with remarkable talents, but not for the likes of me. The longer this situation continued the harder it became for me to extricate myself from it. Eventually, after much deliberation and soul-searching, I reluctantly conceded that my circumstances were unlikely to change and that I was destined to remain where I was indefinitely. I also concluded that I should abandon any hope of progressing further and just accept my lot.

With the knowledge I've gained since then, I now know what was holding me back for so long. I had unwittingly let disparaging, hurtful, offensive and ill-judged comments from my past keep me from realising my true potential; comments such as "You'll never amount to anything", "You just don't have what it takes", "That's not for the likes of you". These negative remarks were dominating my thinking and thwarting my progress. I couldn't shake them off, but instead allowed these detrimental statements to slowly erode my self-confidence. As time went by, I found that I was not only succumbing to these pessimistic opinions, but, worse still, I was echoing these sentiments myself. By doing so, I was throwing away any chance I had to advance.

I, and I alone, was responsible for the situation I was in. I was unable to go beyond my self-imposed limitations and press forward to the next level. I had developed a defeatist mindset, which led to low expectations and poor self-esteem. I thought I would never rise above my current position because I didn't have enough talent. I assumed that I had already peaked and reached my limits in life, and that I would never be more successful.

Again and again I had tried to progress in life, only to hit a brick wall on every occasion. As a result of this, I became discouraged, disheartened and disillusioned. I simply accepted my situation. I felt trapped by my circumstances and had difficulty believing that I could ever break free. I had settled for mediocrity in my thoughts, attitudes and actions. This flawed perspective was blocking the flow and stopping me from fulfilling my potential.

The trouble with negativity is that it works rather like a vortex or a black hole. If you surrender to it, even for a moment, it will engulf you and suck you in. That's exactly what happened to me; I allowed the destructive and spiteful utterances of others to hold me back for years.

Unbeknown to me at the time, I already had the talent, the creativity, the wisdom and the expertise to progress further, but I wasn't utilizing these assets to the best of my ability. It all starts in our hearts and minds. You have to believe you have what it takes. You were created to excel. There's no limit to what you can accomplish in life once you realise what you have on the inside.

I was thinking negatively when I should have been thinking constructively. Instead of looking for ways to achieve my goals, I was searching for reasons and excuses to abandon them. I was harbouring feelings of inferiority and inadequacy. I mistakenly assumed that people who had achieved more than me, or whose earnings exceeded mine, must surely be better than me.

I had to stop dwelling on negative, destructive thoughts that were impeding my progress. I determined to rid myself of the small-minded mentality that was holding me back. I knew that my life was never going to change until I first changed my thinking. This was going to be quite an undertaking. I would be moving into a new phase of my future and moving away from old, established routines. I realised that there might be changes in my life that I wasn't quite ready for, but that they'd be well worth putting up with because of all that they would eventually lead to.

I knew this was my chance to set a new course for the future. It was my opportunity to fulfil a long-cherished dream. Of course, some factors of my daily life would eventually have to alter, almost beyond recognition, if I was to follow a different path. But as long as I was heading down the right road, a happy, acceptable way to reach my destination would ultimately emerge.

Although the task ahead of me seemed overwhelming, I did have one thing going for me. I have always had an inquisitive mind and an insatiable yearning to seek meaning, and gain knowledge, understanding and insight. This need for answers and explanations has compelled me to study the philosophies and teachings of great thinkers, successful entrepreneurs and high achievers, both past and present. What I've discovered has helped me to unearth and utilize a chain of amazing principles that have been responsible for many successes throughout history. After applying these techniques in my own life, my circumstances improved considerably. In fact, so marked has the improvement been that the life I once dreamed about is now a reality.

This book is the result of over eighteen years of extensive research. The knowledge I've gained has provided me with the answers to many of life's big questions. Questions like: Why is one person happy and optimistic while another is forlorn and downbeat? Why is one person rich and successful while another is poverty-stricken and dejected? Why is one person nervous and jittery and another self-assured and relaxed? Why is one person happily married while another has a string of broken relationships?

These and other questions are clearly defined and answered in this book. It was questions like these that drove me to research and write this book, and ultimately discover a completely new way of looking at how to fulfil your greatest desires.

If you're feeling downhearted, there's no need to feel this way any longer, for you are about to discover a few simple principles that will free you from your heartache, disappointment, anxiety, doubt and despair. Once you have incorporated these techniques into your daily routine, you will know how to face up to life's challenges, eliminate your fears and release your potential. You'll find it illuminating, uplifting and inspiring.

You'll learn how to draw on knowledge, skills and expertise you didn't even know you possessed. But like a gifted musician, a fine scholar or a natural athlete, you're never going to lose the magic that makes you special. You've always had what it takes and you've still got it now. Are you equal to the task? Of course. Will you need to go beyond wherever you've been before? Quite possibly. Fulfilling your true potential requires a great deal of determination and self-belief. You must be prepared to step outside of your comfort zone. But, if you truly believe in yourself you will gladly pay any price and go any distance to achieve your goal. Treat the challenge before you as an opportunity to shine, and your inner star won't let you down.

This book provides compelling evidence that what you believe, with absolute conviction, will come to be your reality. You don't believe what you see; rather, you see what you believe. You can have negative views about yourself and your ability, or you can have positive feelings that make you feel good and optimistic about what the future holds. Your beliefs about yourself and your surroundings determine your understanding of the world around you. They affect your memory, your feelings, your attitudes, your desires, your fears, your hopes, your doubts, your energy, your health, your actions, your relationships, and even your everyday experiences.

You have only just begun. You can go a lot further. You can achieve so much more. By reading this book you will have set an important process in motion. It will soon gain momentum. You will see a notable change in your circumstances. One thing will lead to another. Before you know it, you will be reaping your just rewards. Even the objective that seems so deeply desirable, yet which appears so hopelessly unattainable, will begin to look feasible. Get ready to be pleasantly surprised.

# CHAPTER 1
# A NEW YOU

Life is not a series of unconnected events. What you did in the past has fashioned the way you are today. What you do today is creating your future. Our every deed has an impact of some kind, but what about our every thought? Can we be sure, when we entertain an idea, that it is not, somehow, changing the course of our life? Simply by holding a notion in our mind we may be influencing the outcome of an event. With that in mind, you may have to rethink and re-evaluate what various sensitive situations and certain people mean to you. You may be letting a fear or a resentment hold you back. Overcome it. Not only will this shape your future, it will help redefine who you are.

Stop what you are doing for a moment. Take a look back at your life. Are you reluctant to do so? Does it fill you with mixed emotions and cause you to remember things you'd rather forget? If that's the case, then don't. Look straight ahead instead. So tell me, what do you see? Could it, by any chance, be yesterday's unresolved issues resurfacing yet again? If you really yearn to see a brighter future, take another long, hard look at the past. Learn from it. Be prepared to move on from it. And then you definitely will start to enjoy a different (and much happier) tomorrow.

Our attitude towards tomorrow tends to differ according to how we feel about today. That, in turn, tends to depend on how we feel about yesterday. The way to make your future brighter now is to go back to the past and rescue something that has been abandoned. A dream, a vision, a hope, a commitment; it is as real today as it was back then. You have not outgrown it. Today is just yesterday's tomorrow, and yesterday's aspirations are still relevant.

Look to the future, but don't totally dismiss the past. Sometimes by glancing back we're able to find what we have lost. We're able to revisit former episodes and see something new in them. We gain a new perspective that enables us to feel more secure about a matter that has hitherto tormented us. Look back with insight, not ignorance. Here is your chance to move on with fresh hope and inspiration. If you are willing to clear up issues from the past, amazing progress can be made.

Drivers need to know what's behind them. But, more importantly, they need to know what's in front. You should glance back every so often, if only to learn from the past, but your main focus needs to be on where you're going. There are choices you can make about your future direction. To make them astutely and wisely, you must keep your eyes on the road ahead.

You may or may not like the path you have taken throughout your life to get to this point. Nevertheless, when you look back, you can see that path in your memory as a solid, definite route. Hindsight gives us greater clarity. But when we look back at all the happiness and heartache we've endured, one fact remains: what's done is done. The pathway to the future, by contrast, is always bound to seem far more precarious. We never know what tomorrow has in store for us. So, how good will things turn out for you in the future? Surprisingly so, if you focus on the positive. For although big expectations may sometimes lead to big disappointments, they may also, sometimes be highly appropriate. Allow yourself to dream big dreams. Your faith in a better future may well be totally justified.

It's not just fashions and music that change with the times; ideas also alter. You are older and wiser than you once were. You have moved on irrevocably. You can't turn the clock back and suddenly become the person you used to be. Revisit the past for enlightenment and a chance to learn from an old experience (perhaps by seeing it in a new light). Check your facts. Deepen your understanding. And allow yourself to move onward and upward. Draw on your experience of the past now, but remember, the future needs to be different.

You are no longer the person you once were. You have learned many lessons and gained many skills. You have a gift on the inside. You are unique. You are talented. You are creative. You instinctively know how to handle the challenges you face. Your experience is precious and relevant. Life is one long education and we never stop making discoveries. Be more of an observer. Watch. Study. Recognise the hidden patterns. Learn to see life's secret signs. Then reset you own expectations. Be motivated by inspiration, rather than by fear. You have to find courage before you can make a change. Remember, you aren't vulnerable; you're powerful. If you are to see a reversal of fortune, all that needs to change is one person's attitude. Yours!

All of us must learn to put human fallibility into perspective. After all, even those of us who often feel inadequate have to accept that there are limits to our limitations. There are some things we definitely can do well! While those of us who expect perfection (both from ourselves and others) must learn to face up to reality. It's not all about success or failure, but about finding strength, wisdom, insight and tenacity. Once you have achieved this, the best outcome will inevitably ensue.

You really have to make a choice now; but it ought not be too difficult for you. Deep down, you already know how you feel about a certain set of options. It's just that, thus far, your conscious mind hasn't yet caught up with your heart. Your head feels that it dare not commit itself to a plan of action without a greater ability to explain why. Fear not! Once you determine which path you intend to take, good and convincing reasons why you should continue on your course will eventually materialize.

It's a shame that human beings aren't all-knowing or all-seeing. If we were, life would no longer hold any surprises for us, pleasant or otherwise. You do not need the ability to predict every consequence of the plan of action that you are contemplating. You simply need to know whether, on balance, what you're considering is worth pursuing or not. You're afraid of making a bad decision. The truth is, this much insight you do have access to. You've already made the right decision; if it were truly a bad one, you would not even be thinking about it.

You don't have to settle for second best. You don't have to be intimidated or restricted. Above all else, you don't have to feel that you have done something wrong; or that you are in a hopeless situation. Who knows quite why we were created with such a tendency to judge ourselves so harshly? Perhaps it's nature's way of balancing our brilliance and tempering our talent. Now, though, it's time to recognise the full extent of your abilities. You will find that, once you do fully acknowledge the aptitude you possess, others become aware of, and accept it also. The power you seek is the power you already have.

You are capable of far more than you realise. One reason why we tend to use less than our full potential is because we become locked into a stable, but stale, habit pattern. It's all too easy for us to 'coast' through life without stretching our imagination or expanding our horizons. Now is the time to shake yourself out of this trance. You may resent the rudeness of this awakening, but you will never regret the way your life alters as a result. Embrace the new like an old friend! For in an odd way, that's exactly what it is! Indeed, the only thing that is really new about it is your recognition of its existence!

Each of us has a gift, a talent, a rare ability. We were born blessed with this skill, though helpful influences helped us to hone it. It may not represent all that we are, but it forms a considerable part of what we have the potential to become. Don't think of yourself as being small and insignificant. I know this is easier said than done. Even great people have private moments when they feel weak and vulnerable. They may hide their doubts and fears from public view, but they experience them nonetheless. Nothing can impede your progress, except maybe your propensity to be self-critical. Be your own best friend; not your own worst enemy.

What are you capable of achieving? How ingenious can you be when you make the effort? How much knowledge do you have, how much insight have you gained, and what unique talents have you been keeping to yourself? To all these questions, there's just one answer: more than you realise. Deep inside each individual is the ability to summon any resource or develop any skill. This exists within all of us, in much the same way as the potential to become an oak tree lies within every acorn. Sadly, though, many of us do not grow our entire inner tree. Great sections of it perpetually lie dormant, unable to flourish due to a lack of vision and drive on our part. Nourish your inner tree with thoughts of hope, creativity, enthusiasm and advancement. Be inspired. Be motivated. Be imaginative. Be optimistic. Be full of faith. Then somewhere in the heart of your life something wonderful will happen. You will experience the emergence of a power you did not even know you possessed. Start letting the tree of hope grow tall and strong within you. Just remember that powerful positive transformation is a real possibility.

Once you recognise the existence of your inner power, your life will never be the same again. Your life, of course, had plenty of purpose before. Now, though, there's an even more deeply satisfying mission for you to carry out. An objective to aim for. An ambition to fulfil. A fear to confront. A hurdle to surmount. Momentous decisions must now be made, but these can only bring you greater happiness and profound satisfaction. Have courage and be resolute.

# CHAPTER 2
# EXPECT THE BEST

They say that if you want to be successful, you must follow your dreams. This adage applies to a certain extent. But I would be more inclined to say that you should follow your expectations. If you constantly expect the worst to happen, that is exactly what will happen. If you dwell on negative thoughts of inferiority, failure or misfortune, your subconscious mind will do its utmost to bring these experiences into your life. So, by continually thinking limiting thoughts, you are sabotaging your chances of ever reaching a higher level. You will never rise above your expectations. You have to improve your thinking before you can ever improve your life.

From an early age we are taught to lower our expectations. "Don't be silly," our parents say. "You know you can't do that." We are persuaded to set our sights on more practical and less adventurous objectives. It's good that we learn to be sensible, but it's not so good that we also learn to always settle for second best. Life doesn't have to be a succession of regrettable compromises. If you continuously take the safe and reliable option, how will you ever summon the determination required to take your next big leap of faith? Nothing can change for the better until you stop settling for the uninspiring.

What is your definition of success? Is it your level of happiness? Perhaps, if you're not happy at this moment in time it is because you feel you haven't achieved success in a certain area of your life. So, does this mean that you should feel angry or resentful? It's one thing to be focused, another to be obsessed. It's one thing to be driven, another to be ruthless. Watch that you don't blur the line between tenacity and intransigence. It's easier than you think to get what you need the most; it's not quite so easy to recognise what it is that you actually do need. Try to attain the seemingly impossible and you may just achieve some of it. Even if you encounter problems along the way, you'll gain more from believing in miracles than you will from giving up too easily. Just do your best, and trust that if something seems to be taking "too long" it's actually taking the time it needs to take. Don't lower your standards but do alter your expectations. Just wait a while and keep an open mind. All will be fine.

When we have high expectations, we become vulnerable. Yet we do not protect ourselves in any real way by limiting our hopes. You are conscious of what seems like a weakness within yourself. You are afraid of how badly you may be hurt if things go wrong. That is not a reason to give up. It is a reason to be brave, then do your best to be wise. If you pursue noble aspirations, you will get a result that brings great benefit.

When is a failure not a failure? When it leads to a success that could not have come about in any other way. When is a success not a success? When its ultimate outcome results in a failure that might otherwise have been avoided. We are often too rash in our judgement and hastily deem something a success or failure on the basis of a flawed perspective. We apply such terms prematurely. You cannot possibly know whether it is good now to be losing or bad to be winning. Time may well cause you to re-evaluate everything that you think you understand. You do, though, have one infallible way to distinguish the good from the bad. Your instinct. What is it telling you? Pay it some attention. It really does know! If you trust it, it will steer you down the right road.

They say, "You don't know what's possible until you try." Actually, you don't know what's possible until you try, try and try again. Many people are too quick to turn their back on their dreams. They come up with an idea and then exert only a minimum amount of effort to turn it into a reality. They are apathetic and lethargic in their approach. Because of this, at the first sign of any real difficulty, they give up. They don't want to feel embarrassed or, even worse, disappointed. Perhaps there seem to be reasons to abandon an objective. You are just not making the progress you once hoped for. But in your heart, you know you have to give it at least one more shot. Life is full of setbacks and disappointments, but it is also full of successes and rewards. Understand this and be grateful. The way to better your lot is to stop bemoaning it. This is your chance to move forward; to create opportunity where none previously existed. Alternatively, it could also be your chance to go round in circles achieving nothing and feeling sorry for yourself. Stop doubting your ability. If you continue to feel negatively about yourself, you will deflect much of the magic that would otherwise be showered upon you. Have faith.

As long as you just keep doing what needs to be done, you will make the right kind of progress. Sometimes, though, we'd rather do what doesn't really need to be done. Distractions enthral us. Irrelevancies divert us. Conversations distract us and spoil our concentration. All alternatives, no matter how frivolous, seem more appealing than the task in hand. Face your fear. Overcome your apathy. Stay focused. You will find that the further you go down a seemingly difficult road, the more satisfying your journey becomes.

Sometimes we have to do what we don't want to do. Often, when we do this, we discover that it isn't as bad as we feared. We may even come to enjoy the experiences we once dreaded. Too often we waste a lot of time and energy worrying about things we'd be better off just accepting. Trust that people are not trying to make your life difficult; nor are they conspiring against you. Simply realise that some tasks, no matter how unpleasant they may seem, must be done. Then set about doing each job with the expectation that it will lead you inexorably closer to an outcome you have long been yearning for.

Why shouldn't things go well? Why can't solutions fall neatly into place? Is it really fair to blame ourselves for all the problems, complications and setbacks we suffer? Couldn't there be an outside force plotting against us? Actually, no! Most misfortune is of our own making. But the comforting consequence of this is that it is equally in our power to bring good fortune into our lives. Believe that a positive outcome is assured, and you will get one.

The secret of success involves appreciating what you've got. Don't waste time feeling upset if this doesn't fit in with your idea about what you ought to have. Develop an acceptance and appreciation, even for things that have not turned out exactly as you would have liked, and for the people you are in conflict with. Then you will find that, somehow, others direct acceptance and appreciation towards you. You must learn to embrace reality, warts and all. If you regard most things as being good and truly appreciate them, what's bad will get better.

It doesn't matter what you do. It doesn't matter where you go. It doesn't matter what you accomplish. It doesn't matter how much money you have got. Nor does it matter what you know, or what you understand. Or what you think you understand. What matters is how much you believe in yourself.

Be shrewd and think positive thoughts, and then use your discernment. Be amenable, be flexible and be ready to start moving in a new direction. Sometimes, the only way to make something constructive occur is to take a risk. But you'll soon feel proud that you managed to rise to the challenge so well.

Acknowledge and satisfy your cravings for success. But try to take on the sort of challenge that will please you deep down inside.

Aim for the right target and everything you need you'll get.

Are you in danger of going too far? The answer is "probably". But that, on balance, is better than not going far enough. There are points you need to prove, obstacles you need to overcome and changes you sorely need to bring about. If you overstep the mark, you can always retrace a few of those steps. If you don't stride forward, though, while you have the opportunity, you may not get the chance again for a while. Even at the risk of upsetting some people who'd prefer you to be less ambitious and more cautious, you have to trust your bravest instincts and impulses now.

Our circumstances tend to reflect our level of expectancy. Therefore, if you don't develop the habit of expecting positive things to happen, all you're going to experience is more of the same. Low expectation leads to low self-esteem, which in turn leads to a life of mediocrity. Even when your situation looks bleak and you're tempted to feel demoralized or disheartened, you must believe that you have the capacity to triumph over any adversity and there's no limit to what you can achieve. If you anticipate good things coming your way and don't allow yourself to become discouraged or depressed, when the time is right, your situation will turn around.

"There is only one corner of the universe you can be certain of improving, and that's your own self." So said Aldous Huxley. There's not much in the external world that you can easily adjust, but in your inner world, there's a great change that you can bring about. Those two worlds are much more deeply connected than most of us ever realise. Alter your point of view and you'll alter what you are looking at! Convince yourself that you can reach your objective and you'll start to see how that's possible. If there's something you're unhappy about, seek a source of inner strength that doesn't depend on changing circumstances.

Every new day offers us the chance to wipe the slate and start again in some area of our life; and today is no exception. But actually, it is an exception! It doesn't just provide the opportunity to make some small change in your circumstances; it holds forth the hope that you can bring about a significant transformation. Today is as good a day as any to start afresh. You may be uncomfortable about a situation that seems unsatisfactory. You would very much like this to change. That's really not an impossible aspiration. Changing your life, freeing yourself from stress and opening up your heart to joy may not be such an impossible dream. It depends, more than you realise, on how willing you are to alter an old attitude or expectation. That's very much within your power to do.

If you think it will be difficult, or impossible to change your thinking overnight, you are mistaken. Habits are easy to form and hard to break. That's why the best way to change an old behaviour pattern is not to just quit doing it; but to quit doing it and substitute it immediately with a new, more positive practice or habit. If you now focus on a constructive way ahead, you will steadily outgrow a temptation to stay in the same old rut. You don't have to force yourself to do anything, just inspire yourself to seek a solution that will work for you. Remember, you can always neutralise a negative thought by sending out a positive one.

It's time to raise your expectations and lower your inhibitions. Dare to think the unthinkable. You can achieve almost anything if you put your mind to it. But you must know what it is you are trying to achieve. You may be considering a number of options. Instinctively, though, you know which one of your ideas has more merit than the rest. Use your hidden ability to move a mountain and free yourself from a prison.

How different do you think things are going to be in the future? Think again! You have, as yet, no idea just how different they actually will be! Even if you're expecting the best, hoping for the best, or dreaming of the best, chances are your vision will be wonderfully surpassed by the reality. When this occurs you'll feel better inside; because you will, at long last, be overcoming a secret fear. Your improved level of self-assurance will bring forth very tangible new developments in your outer world. Things that have not been possible in the past will slowly but surely become achievable. But you must be ready, willing and able to rise to any half reasonable challenge.

Think big. Be adventurous. Don't dismiss an idea simply on the basis that it seems impractical. Even if you have legitimate misgivings, you can accept the inspiration that accompanies an aspiration or the potential behind a possibility, and, in turn, let this open up doors in other areas of your life. The world is a big place. A lot of magic happens in it. It's not rational to assume that none of this is going to filter through to your world. Deepen your trust and be open to new suggestions; a minor miracle may yet happen.

Whatever you need to overcome you can triumph over. Whatever you have to beat you can conquer. Don't waste vital energy indulging a fear. Nothing can have power over you unless something within you secretly decides to allow this. What you think will happen is probably what will happen. So think positive!

# CHAPTER 3
# DON'T BE DETERRED

Too often we allow negative comments from our past to keep us from pressing forward. We fail to realise that how somebody has behaved towards us, or what they've said about us doesn't change our potential. That capability is still inside us. No human being has control over another. The power someone has over us is only ever the power we allow them to have. Are you blaming someone for a limitation you've chosen to put upon yourself? If so, are you ready to break free from your self-imposed limitations and move on to a new level?

As you climb the ladder of success, many people will encourage and support you. Some will applaud you as they see you ascend. Some will give you practical assistance. They may even move aside so as to make it easier for you to clamber above them. Others may not be quite so selfless and ungrudging, but those individuals will be easy to spot. It's only once you really start openly, obviously winning that people will turn against you and begin to secretly yearn for your downfall. Don't judge and don't be concerned. All you need do is be honest, ethical and sincere. Everything else will then take care of itself. You can rise above negative reaction by reaching for the very best within yourself.

If people are talking about you behind your back, that's great. It means you do not have to listen to them. And you most certainly don't need to be sensitive to your own fears about what people might (or might not) be saying. Think about what matters to you, and why. Also think about what you're prone to take too seriously and allow yourself to get anxious about. Then think about how you, just by thinking differently, can solve a problem, heal a wound, overcome a fear, deepen a bond and have a truly wonderful life.

What will people think? What will people say? Why should you care about what they think, or say? It's amazing how much time and energy we sometimes put into being concerned about appearances. We want to make a good impression, of course. We want to be admired and respected by those around us. We want people to applaud our achievements. But we really don't want to prevent ourselves from doing what we could greatly benefit from doing for fear of being badly thought of. The only judgement you ever need concern yourself with is your own.

The more you do what you feel sure is right, the more likely you are to encounter people who feel sure you're wrong. If, on the other hand, you are foolhardy enough to pursue a course of action that you secretly know to be unwise, you are likely to encounter very little criticism. Only those who are very brave (or very devoted to your well-being) would ever dare say something. Most will either humour you or keep their opinions to themselves. When you see who is raising objections and who is keeping quiet, this will tell you all you need to know.

There is often a delicate balancing act to be performed. You may find it so hard to please someone that you begin to suspect the best you can do is acquiesce and comply with their wishes. This, you surmise, should minimise the risk of causing offence. But even that may be tricky, for elsewhere another person's needs directly opposes those priorities. So, should you just abandon every effort to be popular and honour your own wishes? Yes, but you must psychologically prepare to withstand a small backlash.

If you worry about what others will think of you, you will waste a lot of time, energy and resources. For no matter how hard you try, you will never create a perfect impression in the mind of everybody. Also, you will be overlooking one vital factor. The people you are trying so hard to please are equally keen to please you. If you really want them to think highly of you, simply tell them that you have a high regard for them. This will throw them completely off balance. Sometimes sensitivity and humility are the best weapons to use against intolerance and arrogance; it makes you feel better too. We all have the ability to enhance the lives of those around us. There's always something we can contribute to help others raise their self-esteem and self-confidence; always something we can share. But why should we concern ourselves with other people's needs when we can't even satisfy our own desires? The answer's simple: because of the ancient and unerring 'law of attraction'. Somehow, indirectly but inevitably, we get back what we give out. If there's something you want, the way to get it, at least in part, is to help someone else get what they want.

Someone may want you to think differently. Think twice before you allow them to influence your ideas or alter your opinions. You may be suspicious of this person's motives. It may also suit them if you change your mind and take their advice, but how will it benefit you? Feel free to enter into a discussion with this person. Be open-minded. If you are being listened to, take their advice on board. Then use your discretion as to whether you wish to follow this advice or not. But if you are being talked at, rather than talked to, feel free to ignore whatever is being said.

Certain people may try to stir up feelings of insecurity and uncertainty within you by awakening negative emotions that cause you to doubt your own ability. Overcome this detrimental and harmful frame of mind. Stand firm and resolute. Don't allow anyone to make you feel as though you don't have what it takes, or that your best just isn't good enough. Constantly affirm to yourself: "My best is more than good enough." Do you pay too much attention to people to constantly leave you feeling deflated, dejected and demoralized? Are you settling for mediocrity when you could be achieving brilliance? Is there a part of you that thinks you lack the necessary knowledge and experience to attain your goal? That's simply not the case! You have learnt more throughout your life than you realise. Don't let those who wish to exploit, manipulate or disempower you succeed in their quest to deter you from pursuing an option that is open to you. Be careful whose advice you take, especially if you are being told that something you think is feasible cannot happen. Refuse to sit back and tolerate this situation any longer. For, if you continue to accept it, accommodate it and embrace it, you're never going to rise above it. Break through those limitations of the past and let your mind dwell on thoughts of success, fulfilment and prosperity.

Why assume that someone else knows more than you do; or is somehow more entitled to respect and reward? It is one thing to be naturally modest; another to let this humility develop into an inferiority complex. You are worth a lot more than you realise, both to others and to yourself. You may feel you can only see how far you have left to go; but you should look at how far you've come. You have set in motion a vital process that is bound, eventually, to lead to a most welcome change. Be proud of what you have managed to accomplish. Then reach for what you desire and deserve.

It is one thing to be persuaded, another to be swayed. It is one thing to request advice, another to seek instruction. There's a crucial dividing line you must take care not to cross. Canvass opinion. Acquire information. Consider different points of view. Remember, though, that ultimately you must listen to the voice in your heart that is trying so hard to steer you down the wisest road. It deserves your respect and attention. There's a profound, positive change you can set in motion. You can't base your most important choices on the values, opinions and principles that someone else holds.

We throw away so many opportunities when we make our decisions purely on the basis of whether or not others will approve of them. You need, of course, to be aware of what those around you are likely to think. It is prudent to take this into consideration. But it is one thing to take this into account and another to let it be the reason why you deprive yourself of an entitlement.

People love to give advice. But they don't always stop to consider whether their advice is well thought through or accurate. They just let the words of wisdom pour forth in an understanding, knowledge-able tone of voice. Listen, if you wish, to what is being said; but don't be guided. Remember what you know. There are key factors, which only you have the ability to allow for.

Once you become more aware of what you're capable of achiev-ing, there will be certain individuals who will feel resentful and try to deter you by deliberately undermining your self-confidence. That's because they find it threatening to see someone progressing while their situation remains stagnant. Consequently, they do their utmost to bring others down to their level by planting negative thoughts in their minds. Keep away from people like this and get into an atmos-phere of success, where people build you up rather than knock you down. Find people who will encourage you and inspire you to reach new heights.

The truth is: other people's opinions do not have any bearing on your life. What they say or think about you does not alter what you have inside. Don't allow them to influence your thoughts, because a confused mind will lead you towards lack, resentment, disap-pointment and frustration. Whereas a clear, determined, purposeful, focused mind will bring forth abundance, enlightenment, joy and fulfilment.

What can you do if you really try? You never know until you try. That's when you find out! We all suffer from two conflicting condi-tions. One moment, we are full of confidence and enthusiasm. The next, we are consumed by fear and uncertainty. The latter tends to override the former. If we set our sights too high and then fail, we overcompensate by resetting them at a ridiculously low level. You are capable of doing some truly amazing things. Have faith in your ability and you won't be disappointed.

Some jobs look difficult until you actually get round to doing them. Many tasks seem daunting and intimidating. Sooner or later, though, we know we have to confront them whether we like it or not. Once we get round to tackling them, we soon realise that they weren't so scary after all. The perception was worse than the reality. The thought was more difficult than the deed. If you are apprehensive about the task that lies ahead of you, stop expecting the worst and simply start the process rolling. You'll soon find that it will roll all the way to success.

Somewhere deep within you there's a person of immense power. You're by no means ordinary. On the contrary, you're extremely special. Why, then, don't you act with more of the confidence that you deserve to display? Why don't you accomplish greater things? Why do you let minor setbacks unnerve you? With faith and commitment there is no impediment you can't overcome and no problem you can't solve. Now is your opportunity to reveal what's really within you. You have something truly valuable to offer; the sooner you recognise this, the better.

When you have a talent, you often don't realise how unique it is. To you, it seems ordinary and commonplace. You assume that everyone else is blessed with the same ability. You overlook the fact that others need help to accomplish what comes so naturally to you. You are also totally unaware that, to them, your special gift is greatly prized. Is something being taken for granted somewhere in your world? If so, this isn't a situation that can be allowed to continue. There needs to be acceptance and recognition of your true worth. It's time to hold your head high and dismiss previous doubts that have held you back for too long.

You may be hesitant about taking the risk you are now contemplating. But what if you do? What if it goes wrong? What if you end up looking foolish with a lot to explain? But, then again, what if you don't try? What if you miss out on a golden opportunity? What if you end up regretting your indecision? As long as you follow the first law of gambling you should be okay: never bet a penny more than you can afford to lose. There is a point beyond which you must not go. Until you reach it, you should keep pressing forward. And if it's an emotional gamble, rather than a financial one, remember that pride is never worth trying to maintain.

It's time to make sure you know the difference between what you know, and what you merely think you know. Resist the temptation to make a negative assumption. You may have persuaded yourself that a certain conversation is going to be difficult or that a particular project is likely to prove problematic. The more you find out about what's really going on, the more confident you should start to feel. Stop expecting trouble round every corner. It's not on the way!

Sometimes, things work out wonderfully. Arrangements fall into place. Convenient coincidences crop up. We feel as if we are 'in the flow' and can't put a foot wrong. Then there are times when the opposite occurs. Nothing fits. Everything fails. A wave of despair sweeps over us and we feel like throwing-in the towel. Yet both conditions are, in reality, two sides of one coin. Almost all things can be put right with patience, faith and understanding. If you persevere, you can turn a situation right round.

Have you ever taken on a challenge that, at first glance, seemed insurmountable? How did you cope? What did you do? Try to remember what you did (or what you didn't do) the last time you came under heavy pressure. That will give you a valuable insight into what you need to do now, to extricate yourself from a troublesome situation. It's time to stop being afraid of the power that a particular person or organisation has over you. Refuse to be intimidated by anyone or anything. Don't mistake a sense of uncertainty for a sign of imminent doom. And don't be deluded by your own sense of guilt, fear or some misplaced sense of inadequacy. Be bold and stand your ground and you'll be rewarded with success.

# CHAPTER 4
# THE POWER WITHIN YOU

You view and perceive the world around you by using two distinct segments of your mind. These are often referred to as your conscious and subconscious mind. Your conscious mind is your objective mind because it is solely responsible for receiving information and evaluating whether or not it will be of any use to you. It observes the world and gains knowledge via your five physical senses. It learns by observing, analyzing and interpreting your environment. Your objective mind directs your life; it is the thing that you use to think and reason with. It is your inner voice, the voice you recognise and identify as being you. Although you would be unable to function as a rational, thinking human being without your conscious mind, there are limits to what it can achieve on its own. Whereas your other mind has virtually no constraints on it whatsoever.

Your subconscious mind is commonly referred to as your subjective mind. It is like a huge filing cabinet that contains every thought, opinion, impression, belief, feeling and experience that you've ever had. Your subjective mind is also responsible for the operation of your heart, breathing, circulation and digestion; in fact, all the vital functions of your body. This is all carried out automatically, by a process which enables the subconscious mind to perform numerous tasks without having to think about them.

It acts like a powerful computer, so sophisticated and intelligent that it can execute an innumerable number of duties. Your subconscious mind is your direct link with infinite intelligence, or your higher, all-knowing self. It has limitless knowledge, and will guide you and provide you with all the information and know-how you need to accomplish any goal that you set for yourself.

Your organs continue to function without any conscious effort on your part. Your heart beats, your lungs pump and your stomach digests through processes that are beyond your control. These vital tasks are being carried out by unseen forces. Are they helping you in other ways? Might they be working at other levels? They obviously have your best interests at heart, otherwise they wouldn't be working so hard to keep you alive. Behind the scenes, crucial factors could be working in your favour. You have more help than you think. Let that encouraging thought spur you on to even greater feats.

You are not alone. You have a friend who is constantly striving to give you the peace and harmony you yearn for. This friend does not see some people or situations as more important than others. He responds to sincerity, not status. Who is this friend? Where can you find him? Answer: he is your subconscious (higher self), and you'll find him in the one place you never think of looking, but the one (and only) place where he can ever be found. Put your faith, therefore, in the power that lies within you. If you now want to glow with true joy, light your inner candle. Regardless of what's going on around you, be pure, be strong, be wise, be humble and be happy. And then you'll be naturally guided in the right direction. You have more influential support than you realise.

Recognition of your extraordinary inner power may not come to you after reading this chapter. You may have to delve a little further; it will depend upon your circumstances and what you wish for yourself. Or maybe it will suddenly flash into your mind hours or even days after you have read a certain chapter. But make no mistake; when it comes, you'll recognize it for what it is. It will probably come to you in the form of an idea or a plan. Be on the lookout for this sudden insight. It will probably 'flash' into your mind as an 'inspiration' or a 'gut feeling'. Don't ignore this feeling, but instead act upon it as soon as you receive it. Failure to do so could have far-reaching ramifications. So remember, as soon as you get that inner nudge, you must take immediate action. This is extremely important!

Look out for an apparent mistake that turns out to be a stroke of genius, for an idea based on a misunderstanding but which solves a problem perfectly. Also for circumstances that seem unfortunate yet which are leading to an outcome that is extremely advantageous. Be open to serendipity, to happy coincidences, and to the right things happening, even if seemingly for the wrong reasons. But, most importantly, be aware of incontrovertible proof of a guardian angel working tirelessly on your behalf.

You may find it hard to believe that the subconscious mind is the medium through which you connect with infinite intelligence, but once you accept this concept you'll realise that you have complete control over your future. This mind is the source of all imagination, creativity, insight, ideas and inspiration. It is working ceaselessly to bring about a solution to all your problems and an answer to all your questions. It is set in motion by your overriding concerns, dominant desires or specific plans.

Throughout this book I use the terms subconscious mind, higher self and guardian angel to describe the omniscient force within us. You can call it whatever you want; it doesn't really matter. The important thing is that you become aware of the fact that you are not alone. You are constantly being wisely guided; not by a voice bellowing inside your head, but through your instincts, feelings and insights. It is a force far beyond anything we can even begin to comprehend. Nevertheless, it is always there for you, tirelessly working on your behalf. Just be thankful that you have been blessed with a gift that will always steer you in the right direction.

The moment your subconscious mind accepts any idea or plan, it sets about helping you accomplish it. It draws upon all the knowledge, energy, insight, skill and creativity within you, putting to use every piece of information you have accumulated in your lifetime. Sometimes it appears to achieve immediate results, but there will also be times when it may take considerably longer. Exactly how your subconscious achieves this is beyond our comprehension. All you need to know is: a mental picture held in the mind, backed by self-belief and determination will get definite results.

Thoughts are continually being impressed on your subconscious mind. If you have furnished it with mistaken, inaccurate, hostile or pessimistic beliefs, now is the time to correct that. The most effective way to do this is by repeatedly thinking positive, creative and constructive thoughts, which help to stem the flow of negative influences. Your unlimited potential lies in your ability to control your beliefs about yourself. These beliefs are mostly subjective and not based on facts; nevertheless you have accepted them as true.

If you are dissatisfied, disappointed, disheartened and disillusioned with your life, it may be because you have adopted mistaken beliefs that have hindered your progress. The way you view yourself determines the way you think and act. From now on, positively affirm to yourself what you want to be and where you want to go. Understand that all that really matters is what you are going to accomplish. And what you are going to accomplish is limited only by your self-belief. So, you must develop the belief that you have the potential to accomplish whatever you desire.

If you habitually think positive thoughts, your subconscious mind will readily accept them. Once you understand this, you will have taken the first momentous step towards gaining control over your life. What's more, your constant positive thinking will ensure that no unwanted thoughts can influence your subconscious in any way.

Your subconscious mind does not reason or think for itself. That is the function of your conscious mind. It merely responds to the impressions implanted by your conscious mind. Nor does it decide which course of action to take. It simply accepts whatever information you give it.

The subconscious is all-knowing. As I have previously stated, it has the answer to every question and the solution to every problem. In spite of this, it is still incapable of disregarding any negative thoughts that you impress upon it. Furthermore, it is unable to tell you what thoughts you should be giving it in order to improve your situation; this is the paradox of the subconscious mind.

Your subconscious mind will always respond in accordance with your predominant thoughts. Therefore, if you continually think negative or limiting thoughts, your subconscious will dutifully provide you with these conditions. It does not reason; it simply obeys.

The power of your subconscious mind is immeasurable. It motivates, directs and guides you. It never stops working. Why then, when our instincts are so strong and our inner voice so reliable, do we sometimes make decisions we later come to regret? There could be numerous reasons. Occasionally, we need to 'get it wrong' in order to learn a vital lesson, one that will be of enormous benefit to us. Or it may be because we have an innate tendency to worry about things that need not really concern us. We become so anxious that we end up acting on what we think instead of listening to what we feel. If you have a strong feeling, it may not be easy to rationalise or explain it, but you should still trust it.

If you do not convey specific plans or desires to your subconscious mind, it will pluck out random thoughts and naturally assume that they're the outcome you desire. Bear in mind that thought impulses, both positive and negative, are entering your subconscious continuously through your five physical senses. You are living constantly amongst all kinds of thought impulses, which are penetrating your subconscious mind without your knowledge.

Every thought, feeling, assumption, opinion or idea that you impress on your subconscious mind is stored and recorded. They will eventually turn up in your life as experiences, events, occurrences and circumstances. Whatever you believe on the inside, you will experience on the outside.

Self-talk is the continual conversation you are having with yourself. You develop, alter or adapt your self-image by using words that evoke images that, in turn, stir up a feeling or an emotion. Your self-image is a collection of all the thoughts, feelings and beliefs you have amassed and retained about yourself throughout your life. It is the subconscious image and perception you have of yourself. It influences the way you think and the way you act.

Every time you recall a distressing experience, it becomes embedded in your subconscious and remains there until you make a conscious effort to substitute it with a more favourable image. Therefore, if you wish to improve your self-image, one very effective method is to use self-talk and visualization to form a new image that will bring about the improvements you desire.

Your subconscious believes that all the information you give it is true, irrespective of any evidence to the contrary. If someone says something hurtful to you, that remark makes an impression on your subconscious. Every time you recall this incident, as far as your subconscious is concerned you are going through that experience all over again. Your subconscious cannot differentiate between a real or imagined experience.

This world can be a harsh, cruel place at times. A place in which there are people who, it seems, revel in being cold and disapproving. They aren't happy unless they're belittling or undermining someone. Negativity begets negativity. Bitterness begets bitterness. Contempt begets contempt. Goodwill, fortunately, is also contagious. If you generate positive energy, you can dispel a lot of gloom. Find the courage to be kind. Be strong enough to be soft.

Stand up to cynicism. No matter how weak you may feel, you will ultimately reach a position of power.

Perhaps, like me, you've been told countless times to 'face facts'. Facts, though, have a tendency to change when viewed from a different perspective. It's easy to look at a difficulty and say, "This situation is intolerable. I might as well give up." When you really make an effort, though, you can often make a difference. That's a fact; and one worth bearing in mind! You may be faced with a problem that seemingly cannot be solved. But, no matter how bleak the circumstances may seem, you shouldn't abandon all hope until you have explored every option. You may have an idea about how to put right this situation, but you fear that it is a little foolhardy and irresponsible, that others will disapprove or that they will scoff and urge you to 'face facts'. Conventional wisdom won't steer you in the right direction, but intuition and inspiration will!

Deep down we know what makes sense. For some reason, though, we're often afraid to follow what we feel. Either we doubt our ability to do what we want or we fear that something might go wrong. So we are inclined to consider what seems like a safer option, albeit one that involves a compromise. It's not that this modified solution won't work. It probably will. But it won't give you the result you deserve. Only if you aspire to the best will you get it.

# CHAPTER 5
# ALTER YOUR OUTLOOK

Minds were made for changing. People who form an opinion and then stick to it rigidly are either narrow-minded or foolish. Strangely, though, we often feel embarrassed and ashamed to confess that we have come to see a situation in a different way. We should, though, feel proud that we have developed enough wisdom to outgrow a former position. Although, if we are truly wise, we will not be proud, just quietly humble! Embrace a new perspective. Explore a new point of view. Be willing to adapt and then be ready to benefit.

You are a human being; you have your flaws and shortcomings, just as you have your talents, strengths and insights. It is important to remember that, even if you are not perfect, you have nothing to be scared of, and everything to look forward to. You are a mere mortal and are, therefore, prone to making the occasional mistake. But, as long as you acknowledge this reality and remain willing to learn, you will be guided well. Look for, and find, the divine in all things. In a seemingly ordinary situation, something magical may be happening. Be aware of this! Forget whatever makes you feel fearful. Trust whatever inspires you.

Be glad of everything that makes you feel discontented. Be grateful for every cause of complaint. How, without this, are you ever going to enjoy the satisfaction of putting things right? Do not doubt your ability to work such miracles. You can, if you relax, bring forth a very real, natural magic. Whatever you do, do it wholeheartedly. The only 'wrong thing' you can do is be afraid.

The world is full of deeply intuitive, illogical and emotional beings attempting to pretend that their actions have a perfectly rational explanation. The mind is quick but the heart is quicker. First, we feel something. Immediately after, we conjure up a convenient rationale for why we feel it. It is never the other way around. Even so-called intellectuals are governed by this law. No matter how wise we may be, our cover stories rarely reflect true motives behind our deeds and actions.

How can you know where you are going if you don't understand where you have been? It is time for you to rewrite history. You need to look back at some of the experiences that have shaped and moulded your life. Though you may feel you understand the lessons you've learned from these events, your perspective may have become distorted. You have revisited certain incidents from your past over and over again in your mind so many times that you've overlooked the possibility that there could be another version of the story. Could there possibly be another way to see it? Reinterpret yesterday; change tomorrow.

There are circumstances in which it is wiser to lose a battle. Sometimes, we get so caught up in our desire to fight that we forget what really matters to us. We decide we must have victory at any cost. We become so enraged by an injustice or so determined to avenge an insult that we lose all perspective. Don't overreact. Don't take umbrage at a slight slight. Don't get up on your high horse and don't start seething with rage. Unless, that is, you want to. You're a free spirit. If that's what gives you pleasure, go ahead. But, if you've had enough of intense experiences, you can opt for a path that will lead you to a calmer, more prosperous and far less troublesome future. You have a lot of power at your disposal. Think carefully about the most effective way to use it.

Could you have misjudged something or someone? As events take you back over old ground, they cause you to re-examine your ideas and appraisals. Be big enough to acknowledge and apologise for any errors. Don't worry about losing face. The bottom line is: you are laying the foundations for a brighter future; that's what counts.

As you strive to move forward, there will be times when it seems as though, no matter where you turn, you come up against a restriction or impediment of some kind. A physical difficulty, or a psychological one. All this may be frustrating, but you have to confront an obstacle before you can overcome it. Before you can conquer your demons, you must first face them.

Firstly, stop listening to the people who seem to think you are doing something wrong. Secondly, stop paying so much attention to your inner critic. Then, try to hear a different set of messages. A wiser voice is steering you towards a course of action it would be advantageous to follow. Your intuition wants to help you get on the best possible path. But until you stop feeling so defensive, apprehensive or anxious, you'll keep getting in your own way!

What can't you do? Where can't you go? Why can't you get what you so deeply desire? As you ponder these questions, please consider the possibility that some of these may not be someone else's fault. It could be that you secretly have more reservations and inhibitions than you have been willing to acknowledge. That's not necessarily a bad thing. Sometimes, it's wise for us to hold ourselves back. It is, though, never wise to blame some other person or situation for an obstacle that we have, ultimately, managed to place in our own path.

It can all be so very different from now on. Imagine you are somehow getting what you want and what you need. Your wishes are being granted, hopes being fulfilled. A few minor obstacles still stand in your way, but they are nothing when compared to the outstanding progress you are making. Now, stop imagining and consider your reality. If you think there's a difference it is only because you are unable to see past those obstacles. If, though, you are prepared to honestly explore your deepest fears and aspirations, you will soon discover a way to turn a major barrier into a minor hurdle. You are being wisely guided from within. Your subconscious (higher self) has the solution to all your problems.

You have a brain crammed with thought, a heart full of feelings, and a body laden with physical needs. But, you are also blessed with a spirit, endowed with all the wisdom of the infinite, nestling unassumingly at the core of your very being. This deep, vital part of you doesn't vie for your attention like all the other parts of your persona tend to do. But don't let its quiet demeanour fool you; it has the potential to dramatically enhance your life. With this in mind, don't you think it would be a good idea to acknowledge and consult this inner fountain of knowledge; and then be guided by what it wisely (albeit subtly) advises. Trust your intuition and ignore your doubt.

What does your intuition tell you? Or can you not hear it over the sound of a fear, a misgiving or a sense of foreboding? These feelings may not be justifiable or rational, but when we're experiencing them, they drown out everything else. Yet if we can remain calm, composed and quiet, we will be able to hear a voice from within that speaks with wisdom rather than emotion. Something deep inside you knows what's appropriate to say, do and choose. Locate that sense and trust it.

Too many of us deny our instincts. We're reluctant and ashamed to admit the full extent of our perception. Thus, we end up in the undesirable position of pretending our conscious, logical thoughts are all we need to achieve our desires; and that only a naïve simpleton would contemplate the existence of an unconscious, intuitive presence. A little voice is whispering wisdom in your ear. It deserves your respect and attention. Let powerful passions rise within you once more. Let your heart rule your head. Thankfully, your heart is far wiser than your head. And, ultimately, it is more intelligent, too. Be less sceptical and more open-minded.

When your inner voice speaks, you should listen, pause, reflect, and then comply. Instead of trying to make sense of such events, just accept them for what they are; because the more you try to understand them, the more confused you will become. They cannot be rationalized. There is no logical explanation for them. Some things in the world just happen because they need to happen. They exist to be experienced, not understood. Forget what you think; trust what you feel, and act. Then just watch a threat fade away magically.

You're special. You're unique. You're gifted. Not all the rules of this world need apply to you in the same way they apply to others. I'm not suggesting you have carte blanche to flout authority or do everything your way, but it is important you don't allow yourself to be hemmed in by narrow ideas and unimaginative expectations. You've got ideas that deserve to be taken seriously, dreams that can come true if you wake up and start working on them. Be sensitive to your critics and tactful with those who aren't feeling as adventurous. Seize the moment and be brave. There is no better time than now to explore your options, broaden your horizons and increase your power.

It doesn't take much to turn something pointless into something precious. When, though, you have felt frustrated for a long time by an inability to instigate change, you tend to forget that it is ever possible. There may be something advantageous you can take from your situation. All too often, we overlook the obvious. We get so caught up in what we can't do that we forget about what we can. When we allow frustration to infuriate us, we cloud our consciousness. Clarity is replaced by confusion. From then on, the easiest things begin to seem difficult. How do we turn all that around? Simply by wanting to. If you seek an awakening and a positive change in your circumstances, you will find it makes its way to you simply because you've reached for it.

# CHAPTER 6
# CHOOSE YOUR THOUGHTS CAREFULLY

Why can't you attain your deepest desires? Stop! Don't even attempt to answer that, it's a rhetorical question. What's more, if you do try to unravel this mystery, you will merely be bolstering the obstacles that stand between you and your goals. Every time you list reasons why progress cannot be made, you will drum those difficulties deeper into your subconscious mind. Therefore, don't ask why something can't happen, ask why it can. Better still, ask how it can. If you make enough effort, with enough faith, you'll be amazed by what you accomplish.

We all want the best. None of us, though, want to end up disappointed. That's why we aspire no further than the best we think we're capable of attaining. We put any other thoughts to the back of our mind. We persuade ourselves that, even if we achieved greater success, we wouldn't really enjoy it. That's a shrewd self-protection mechanism, but it has one fundamental flaw. It means that when an opportunity arises to accomplish more, we tend to disregard it. Don't limit your options. Your liberation from limited thinking lies in your ability to control your thoughts. When you control your thinking, you also control your life. Your thoughts and feelings trigger your actions and responses and ultimately determine the results you achieve.

A major failing in many people is the tendency to judge everything and everybody according to their own opinions and beliefs. Such people seem to thrive on pessimism, which is the root of all misfortune. They habitually think in terms of poverty, misery, ill-health and failure. These downbeat people constantly look on the dark, dreary and depressing side of life. Even good times hold some bad for them. They have a pessimistic and cynical attitude towards just about everything. They dwell on the gloomy and negative. They always think something bad is going to happen to them. They harp on about it, anticipate it, expect it, and ultimately, encounter it. It should come as no surprise that they eventually experience what they've been predicting all along.

Negative people spread gloom and despondency. Each day you can observe these individuals as you pass them in the street. No happiness or good will emanates from them; only bitterness and hostility. Having created their own misery, it seems they're intent on sharing it with everybody they come into contact with.

We all know individuals who just aren't happy unless they are complaining, criticising, creating conflict or courting confrontation. Secretly, they take a perverse pleasure in whipping up animosity, hostility and friction. It's difficult, when we encounter such characters, not to sink to their level. It is as if they create a vacuum that draws us in. Steer clear of people who exhibit unnecessary negativity.

Why do some people fill us with enthusiasm, while others evoke feelings of dread? Why are we drawn towards particular individuals and repulsed by others? Our responses are irrational. None of us fully understands our own deepest emotions. If you are having a strong reaction to someone, you must try to fathom why you feel as you do. The more willing you are to do so, the more you will learn about yourself.

It's incredibly easy to let negative thoughts slip into our minds, in much the same way as we let addictive junk food slip into our mouths. Positive thoughts can be harder to unearth. They often require a little effort, but if you seek a better, more enlightened perspective, you must be willing to go further to meet your needs. You don't have to go far to find a person who is cynical, spiteful or surly. These people will happily encourage you to feel and act as they do. But, if you know what's good for you, you'll seek out more constructive company.

Why are some people more popular than others? It is probably because they treat people with respect. If we are nice, others find it harder to be nasty to us. If we are generous, we discourage selfishness; maybe not every time, but more often than not. But there is another benefit to manifesting goodwill. When you do it, you feel better about yourself. Don't be eager to find fault. Look for something to praise in others. Then people will find you more praiseworthy too.

You will only be successful if you are prepared to abandon your limited thinking. If you've been experiencing failure, deprivation or turmoil, it is often due to negative beliefs you have formed about yourself. Therefore, to realise your full potential you must break free from this damaging practice by rejecting all the adverse beliefs that have prevented you from achieving what you're capable of achieving.

Pleasurable or troublesome? Which word more aptly describes your present situation? Life will always confront us with difficulties and annoyances. When, though, we start to feel engulfed by setbacks and misfortune, we lose more than our drive and enthusiasm; we also lose our sense of perspective. We start to think that this is what our existence is all about, and this causes us to focus on our perceived limitations. It's time for you to liberate yourself from these debilitating thoughts, otherwise you're condemning yourself to a life of lack and despondency, or, worse still, bitterness and resentment.

Successful people are very clear about their principles, intentions and aspirations. They ceaselessly look for the positive in every situation. Their whole approach to life, people, relationships, work and money is decisive, ethical and fair. As a result, they are people that others look up to and admire.

You too can become optimistic about yourself and your prospects, and in return you will become a happier and more productive person. But, before you can make permanent and drastic changes to your life, you must understand the power of your thoughts and words.

Each one of us has inner conversations with ourselves throughout every day. In fact, we talk to ourselves more often than we realise. We tend to do this subconsciously, without even knowing that we are doing it. But, what you must ask yourself is: What is your inner voice saying? Are you being fed positive, supportive, empowering statements? Or are you hearing negative, defeatist, confidence-eroding, energy sapping comments?

How you tackle any situation is linked directly to which voice you choose to listen to, and, more often than not, the negative, pessimistic voice overpowers the positive, optimistic utterances. That unfortunately is why we allow ourselves to be held back on so many occasions. Simply because a niggling voice inside our head is saying: "Don't even attempt to do that, you'll only make yourself look foolish. Everyone will laugh at you when you fail. Anyway, you know you haven't enough talent."

By contrast, the vast majority of us don't pay enough attention to our empowering voice, which urges us to push ourselves further with inspirational statements like: "Go on, what have you got to lose? You can do it. You definitely have what it takes to achieve that."

Positive affirmations can enrich your life. Constructive thoughts have the power to boost your strength and confidence. They also have a beneficial affect on your state of mind, health, energy levels and enthusiasm. They help you unlock your potential and bring forth the genius that is lying dormant within you. When this happens, you will feel excited and passionate about the ideas that are being created in your mind. The more ideas you create, the more excited and passionate you will become. You will feel self-assured and courageous, and you will know that you have the potential to achieve more than you ever dreamed possible; and that whatever you've achieved up until now is nothing compared to what you'll achieve from now on.

Negative assertions are life-depleting. They inhibit you and drain your energy and confidence. They leave you feeling irritable and anxious. Eventually they can have a detrimental effect on your health and state of mind. Your ability to perform even the simplest of tasks is severely diminished, which leaves you feeling angry and defensive.

It is extremely important to remember that every time you think or say something negative, you're actually harming yourself. Bearing this in mind, the eradication of negative thoughts is the most beneficial single step you can take if you want to enjoy good health, happiness and peace of mind. As you learn to take control of your thoughts and feelings, and keep them positive at all times, the quality of your life will significantly improve. So, if you want to live a rewarding life, your aim should be to habitually think positive thoughts and relinquish all negative thoughts.

The power of these inner voices is immense. Therefore, it follows that you should closely scrutinize your internal dialogue. Remove all negative phrases from your vocabulary. If you choose to listen to the wrong messages, it will hamper you for the rest of your life. Whereas, if you talk to yourself in the right way, you'll not only enjoy life more, but you'll also rise to a new level of expectancy and a much more realistic understanding of your abilities, leading to future success. Express positivity and you will attract positivity.

If you continually dwell on what's wrong in your world, you

won't make anything any better. Even if you resolve one difficulty, you'll just end up inadvertently creating another. For, by adopting a pessimistic attitude you will be invoking the universal law of cause and effect; in other words, a self-fulfilling prophecy. If you habitually focus on the downside of every situation, you are as good as inviting problems, difficulties and misfortune into your life. If you convince yourself that something bad is bound to happen, it is more likely it will. Can you provide a logical evidence-based justification for your fears? The evidence to support your feelings of foreboding is, in all probability, flimsy. It seems credible until you investigate it closely, then it begins to fall apart.

Your mind is only capable of holding one thought at a time. You can replace a negative thought with a positive affirmation whenever you want. You can apply this technique by consciously thinking positive thoughts whenever you wish to neutralize a thought or feeling that makes you angry or distressed.

One wrong move could have disastrous consequences. Or so you think. What makes you imagine your path from here to success is so precarious? Why see it as a rickety old rope bridge teetering over a ravine when it is really a sturdy walkway straddling a tranquil lake. If you slip, you can still clamber back on track and ultimately reach your destination. What I'm trying to say is: the stakes are not as high as you fear. The potential for disaster is not as great as you might suspect. On the contrary, you are safe to stride forward with confidence.

## CHAPTER 7
# OPEN YOUR MIND

Did you ever hear the story about the man who, at the end of his life, finally gets to meet his guardian angel? "I've always been with you," says the angel and shows him a picture of his entire life. "Behold," says the angel. "See my footprints on the sands of time, alongside yours?" The man looks, and notices that, during the most painful, sad and distressing periods of his life, there is only one set of footprints in the sand. He turns to the angel and asks, "What about here? That was a terrible time, yet there is only one set of footprints. Why did you abandon me when I needed you most?" "Abandon you?" says the angel. "It was during these difficult times that I carried you." You are not alone.

Guardian angels don't exist. Wish-granting fairies are just the product of a vivid imagination. The universe never singles any of us out for preferential treatment. Science has clearly shown that life is just one long struggle for survival. No 'benign force' has any influence on us. Or does it? No matter what you believe (or refuse to believe), a protective force of some description is looking over you. Do what you can to help it by helping yourself; you'll find the results truly amazing.

Coincidences happen every day. Most of these, though, go unnoticed. They happen to other people; or they happen to us, yet somehow we take them in our stride and never give them a second thought. If we only knew how many guardian angels were toiling day and night to help us, we'd never again complain about difficult issues or stressful situations! Don't doubt the existence of magic in your life. You've got more support than you know.

Want to know how to gain true wisdom? It involves a mixture of compassion and sincerity. If you really mean what you say, and you mean it for the kindest possible reasons, you will end up doing the wisest thing, even if you do it in the most ill-judged way imaginable. Conversely, you can be as tactical and as practical as you wish to be, but if your heart is cold and cynical, the ultimate outcome of your endeavour will profit nobody, least of all you. No matter what pressure you face, be sensitive.

The first steps along the pathway to success can be hesitant and unnerving. There will be times when you doubt your ability and wonder if you're doing the right thing. We've all been there. Many thoughts will go through your mind. "What if I go down the wrong road? What if I make a decision that I later come to regret?" The simple answer is, you will not do either of these! Take a good, hard look at the opportunity that now lies before you. View it objectively, but be open to 'higher guidance'. Instinctively, you'll get it right. You'll see there is only one rational course of action. This requires some courage, and some faith, too, in your own judgement. But why should you not have that? As long as you are diligent, a successful outcome is assured.

Why is it so essential for a process to have a specific outcome? Are you sure you know how things need to turn out? What if you've misunderstood something or are searching for an outcome that's likely to prove problematic? Don't be too quick to assume you know whether you are winning or losing. You're probably nearer than you think to where you need to be. Indeed, it's largely the fact you're thinking too much that's holding you back.

How difficult is your task? Some people may think it is daunting and complicated. This is either because they don't understand it fully or they want you to engage their help. Actually, though, you need little, if any, assistance. If you gather information and overcome your fear of the unknown, you will manage to do all that you feel obliged to do. Instinctively, you already know what's needed. If you are worried that you may get into trouble, persist until the trouble actually arises. There's a good chance that it will loom in the distance but will never actually approach you.

You instinctively know what's best for you. Though you will never be able to hear that distant voice from within if you are experiencing anxiety. Success relies on your ability to be humble, yet confident; quiet enough to hear what your heart is saying, calm enough not to be swayed by fear, yet brave enough to act on whatever seems most appropriate at a deep, intuitive level. Nobody can tell you what to do, but you can tell yourself. Listen to your own deepest wisdom and you'll find out what you're truly capable of achieving.

Like a distant, barely audible voice, trying to attract your attention, something is calling you. From somewhere deep within, a signal is bring transmitted. A message is being sent. Your instincts are trying to tell you something. Or forewarn you of something, but what? The trick is to tune in somehow to your inner voice of wisdom. It's easy to ignore it. It won't kick up a fuss if you do. But what is that elusive memory that you can't quite recall and can't quite shut out? And what is it suggesting about a certain situation? Trust your instincts and you really will begin to tap into a fountain of wisdom.

You don't need to be a genius to figure out how to make the best decisions. You just need to listen to your inner voice. Heed it, trust it, follow it and see where it takes you. In the unlikely event that a powerful urge leads you down a road you really feel uneasy about, you can engage your discerning faculties and look for more practical strategies. More often than not, though, your route to significant progress involves trying to think less, control less and have more confidence in your intuition. How do you differentiate between intuition and wishful thinking? You can't. But with an open mind, plus some wisdom, you won't need to!

Sometimes our instincts are uncannily accurate. We don't have to stop and think because we 'just know' which direction we need to go in. When we are worried, though, we can't hear our inner voice so clearly. We tend to reach for whatever seems most safe and reassuring, even if it involves rejecting opportunity. As sure as night follows day, there will be days when you are under pressure. To free yourself from whatever appears to be creating a problem, you may need to make what may seem like a counter-intuitive move. Try walking closer towards (rather than further away from) a source of trouble. That's not being reckless and foolhardy, it is being brave and far-sighted. Confront a fear, don't cower beneath it.

Do you know that you are endowed with an amazing ability? Deep down, you probably did. You just didn't want to admit it. Nevertheless, it guides you from deep within, blessing you with wonderful insights and visions from time to time. When it's at its maximum capability, you can't just read minds, you can change them!

Fantasies! Don't they just sap our strength and take up our time? Aren't they an unnecessary distraction because, when we finally have to face reality, we realise we could have spent that dreamtime doing something more constructive? There is, though, one good reason why we should allow ourselves a little escapism. Visions are the gateway to the imagination. In that realm, some very real solutions to some very real problems may be found. Don't be too quick to dismiss a fleeting thought or a whimsical notion as a plan you could never act on.

Many people will testify to the power of positive thought. How, though, can our aspirations really alter our reality? Surely, if a situation arises due to circumstance, we must address it through a physical course of action, not merely an attitude. Open your mind and make allowance, from this moment onwards, for the idea that not everything in life has to be sensible. Don't dismiss a silly notion too hastily. The right outlook will help us find the right path. On its own, an affirmation will change nothing. But if you make it, and then start looking for an opportunity, you will find one.

You've got everything you need to succeed. Whenever we lack a resource, we think we'll never get as much done as is needed. That is not the case. You just have to make good use of what tools you have at your disposal. You must simply use what you've got wisely. A small step today could produce a big result tomorrow. Whenever you feel as though your options are limited, consider the possibility that you have just enough for what's required.

How creative can you be? What solutions can you come up with? More than you could ever imagine, if the truth be known. It's possible to see something that has previously been hidden. Secrets can be revealed and codes can be cracked. Your subconscious mind has known, for some while, the best way to solve a particular problem. Now is the time to allow this information to reach the forefront of your awareness. Simply relax and open your mind.

Why attempt the impossible? Because you can't know whether it is impossible until you try! And even if you fail, you may learn something you couldn't have otherwise discovered. There may be numerous reasons to aim for something more practical. But one good reason to proceed with an ambitious objective outweighs them all. What is that reason? Your entitlement to a life that's both exciting and rewarding!

Do you know your limitations? Can you only expect to accomplish a certain amount? Why is that? Don't you think you've got what it takes to excel? It is difficult to succeed when you expect failure. Equally, a belief that something is possible will go a long way towards making it so. Generally speaking, the trick in life is to expect the best outcome. Are you entitled to such a belief? Absolutely!

# CHAPTER 8
# CHANGE YOUR WAY OF THINKING

The way you see yourself determines your feelings and assumptions about what you're capable of achieving. These images are responsible for everything that happens to you. All your actions, emotions and attitudes are formed by this perceived image. You literally take on the identity of the person you imagine yourself to be. What you need to bear in mind is that, if you continue to hold onto this image, you will never change the way you are; you will always act according to the way you see yourself

The one thing in your life that you have complete control over is your thinking. Nobody can tell you what to think. You alone decide what you are going to think at any given moment. These thoughts, beliefs and opinions generate feelings, either positive or negative. Your thoughts and feelings influence your actions and determine how much you achieve. Your subconscious then produces images and emotions that correspond to these thoughts and feelings. These images and emotions prompt attitudes and behaviour that can either help or hinder your chances of success.

If you constantly think about success and achieving positive results, you will feel confident and self-assured, and you will perform to a far higher standard. Whereas, if you think about failure or rejection, you will perform badly, regardless of how competent you really are.

Remember, your mind can only hold one thought at a time. This means you can switch from a negative to a positive thought whenever you wish. You can apply this principle by consciously focusing on something positive when you want to neutralize any thoughts or feelings that are harmful or distressing.

When you habitually behave and act in a confident and constructive manner, you exert total control over your conscious mind. Before long it becomes completely natural and instinctive to think and react in that way, and with self-discipline and determination you can change the way you think and act. When you change the way you think you change the way you live, sometimes instantaneously.

You can acquire any habit or technique that you deem beneficial or essential. Moreover, you can develop positive attitudes towards money, people, health and relationships; because negative thoughts about any of these can severely impede your progress. Likewise, if you detach yourself from people or circumstances that make you feel angry or distressed by refusing to think about them, the negative feelings associated with them will eventually die away.

It is one thing to feel unhappy because something in your world is genuinely bad, disappointing or distressing. It is another to feel down because you don't feel you're entitled to feel any other way. Have you been inflicting unnecessary punishment on yourself? Is there a part of you that half-expects things to go wrong? If so, you have been inviting misfortune and regret into your life. You need to conquer that pessimistic side of you, otherwise you will continue to experience negative results.

Often, people allow their viewpoint to deceive them into thinking that they're useless, incapable, stupid, lazy, bad and unworthy. This inevitably leads to poor self-esteem and poor self-image. Unless you make a conscious effort to change the way you think, you will continue to accept and sustain this false belief. First and foremost you should accept yourself for who you are; in other words, be true to yourself. Learn to accept yourself even with all your faults.

You begin the process of changing your way of thinking by altering your self-image. You form a clear, constructive, inspiring and exhilarating vision of yourself that conforms to the very best person you can imagine yourself to be. You picture yourself performing to your very best ability in everything you endeavour to do. Ultimately you develop such a high level of self-belief that you can take on any challenge with complete confidence.

Do you have any more entitlement to success or happiness than anyone else? This may be the question you frequently ask whenever you feel inclined to assert yourself, or strive to fulfil a burning ambition. The answer is irrelevant, as the question can just as easily be turned around: do you have any less entitlement to success or happiness? You are not in your current situation by mistake; but you'll be making a mistake if you don't see this. Hold on to your faith in a better, brighter future and you'll soon see clear evidence that this is something you definitely deserve.

How you judge yourself influences your behaviour; and the way you behave has a direct bearing on the results you get. When you judge your worth by how well you perform or behave, you're bound to end up feeling bitterly disappointed and dejected. Remember, you can't please everybody; somebody is always going to regard you as a failure, no matter how hard you try or how well you do. Your success in life has got nothing to do with winning people's approval. If someone thinks you're worthless, so what! Simply accept that you'll always be wrong in someone's eyes, and move on. So, given that you can't please everyone, always ensure you please yourself and be proud of who you are.

When you absolutely accept that you are a thoroughly good, decent, hardworking, honest and intelligent person, you will exhibit this in every aspect of your life. Ultimately, you will come to accept that you are an excellent person, and that great success and happiness is destined for you.

You begin the process of releasing your potential and accomplishing even greater things by challenging the beliefs that restrict and suppress your progress. These beliefs cause you to feel inadequate or lacking in a specific area. Even though these beliefs are rarely true, if you accept them as accurate estimates of your ability, you consider them to be so.

You liberate yourself from restricting beliefs by affirming to yourself that they are completely false. Then you visualize having no limitations whatsoever on your abilities. See yourself in your mind's eye having, being and doing anything you want. Imagine that your potential is unrestricted and unwavering. Imagine yourself living in a bigger house, driving your dream car, or enjoying a more extravagant lifestyle. Simply see yourself living life to the full. Think of yourself as being relaxed, confident, decisive and undaunted by anything. Picture yourself being able to accomplish any goal you set yourself.

The better the way you think, the better the way you live. Every internal thought and image triggers feelings, attitudes and opinions; they even affect the way other people react and behave towards you. Therefore, a positive self-image is essential if you are to change your life for the better.

Improvements to any area of your character or temperament build up your levels of self-esteem and self-regard. They cause you to change the opinion you have about yourself. You come to like and value yourself much more. This in turn enhances your self-image and ultimately your performance. You become more like the person you want to be.

When you dislike yourself for what you have or haven't achieved, or feel hostility towards others for what they've done to you, you're into martyrdom. Playing the role of the victim is a way of discrediting and degrading yourself. This all stems from feelings of resentment and disappointment about not living up to your own, or someone else's expectations.

When you reproach yourself for something that you didn't accomplish, or something that didn't go according to plan, or for a situation where you feel you let someone down, you tend to feel bad about yourself. This misguided assessment of the situation will only serve to erode away your self-esteem. It does you no good: but plenty of harm.

We have all said or done things in our lives that we now regret, but there comes a time when you must stop dwelling on these incidents and move on. That time is now!

# CHAPTER 9
# PLEASE YOURSELF

What sort of person should you try to be? Is there a definitive answer? Of course not. Different people in your world want you to act according to their needs and expectations. Try to please one individual and you may well end up upsetting another. Therefore, you should do what pleases you, so long as your motives are sincere and honourable. If you do what you do for the right reasons, you need not worry about what anybody else thinks.

By taking the responsibility for your own life, you're bound to make some people angry, resentful, envious and bitter towards you. Living life on your own terms can sometimes be a very lonely experience, and you may sometimes feel that everyone is against you. But you must be true to yourself and not worry about the opinions of others. Your main concern should not be to do what's popular; but to do what's right.

Sometimes other people's values and beliefs will differ from yours, and when they see your way of living coming into conflict with theirs it makes them feel uneasy, because they have to question their own fundamental beliefs. They have to ask themselves "Who's right? Them or me?" A person who is confident about who they are doesn't feel threatened by other people's values or beliefs.

If you believe that someone is not giving you the recognition you deserve, you can feel hurt and offended, and want to hurt them back. You consider their behaviour to be a personal attack on you as a person, and it leaves you feeling angry and resentful.

Nearly everything we do is designed to build up our confidence and sense of worth, or to prevent ourselves from being ridiculed or undervalued by others. If you have low self-esteem, you will be more sensitive to the way that people behave towards you. You will tend to take things more personally.

Much of what we do in life is driven by our need to either gain or maintain the respect of people that we look up to. These people ultimately determine how well we feel our life is functioning and how satisfied we are with our overall performance.

When we are overly concerned about our social standing, we become disempowered. By caring too much about how we may be judged, we grow dependent on approval and applause. The integrity of our individuality is compromised. We must, of course, be aware of people's feelings; and sensitive to them. That doesn't mean, though, that you should allow yourself to be coerced into making a bad decision.

Should you do this or should you do that? Who will you please and who will you upset? Where should you go, what should you do, when should you change your plans on someone else's behalf? These and other pertinent questions are bound to arise. When they do, remember that you are not obliged to know the answers. You are certainly not obliged to accept conclusions that others think you ought to be reaching. Try trusting what you truly feel, and draw comfort from the knowledge that you are embarking on a journey of self-discovery.

Successful people know exactly who they are, and who they're not; they feel no need to seek the approval or respect of others. Although they take other people's opinions into consideration, in the end they rely solely on their own judgement. They're not really concerned about whether or not they have the consent of others. They instinctively know when they have made the right decision.

You should also act this way.

Seemingly, there are always wiser ways. Sensible alternatives. Things you could or should have done differently. Certain fault-finding individuals are always keen to remind us of this. We all know people who like to pass judgement on those around them. They may be very clever, but they're not very sensitive. Their comments undermine our confidence. We'd rather they kept their opinions to themselves. Especially when they state the downright obvious. We are quite capable of being self-critical when the need arises. We don't need any assistance from opinionated self-appointed overseers. Whose standards should you employ to determine whether something is good or bad? Yours, of course, not somebody else's. Don't worry about making a bad decision, given that, from something bad, something good can often emerge.

You may have friends in high places. You almost certainly have friends with high hopes and high ideals. Do some seem a little too keen to claim the moral high ground? Are others adopting an overly high-and-mighty attitude? If it weren't for the people you know and their influence, life might be less stressful. It might also, though, be less satisfying. Don't allow anyone to judge you too harshly and don't take a particular person's viewpoint too seriously. Among your acquaintances, there's bound to be one with sincerity and wisdom. That's the person to grow closer to!

If you have a plan that you really believe in, but which others seem doubtful about, don't stop believing in it yourself. Sometimes we just need to show others that we have the courage of our convictions. That we won't be swayed by other people's opinions or concerns. But these doubters are not the real danger to us. They can be overcome with determination and tenacity. The really menacing sceptic is the voice of doubt in the back of our own mind. Once you overcome that, you're home and dry. Your current idea is a good one. Stick with it, even if you feel it is being seriously challenged.

You can only be yourself. This may seem like a patently obvious statement, but you'd be amazed at the number of people who fail to recognise this simple fact. This being the case, why then do we sometimes feel inclined to emulate the examples of others? Or even to assume that their ideas and actions are worth more than our own? Without becoming arrogant, and whilst remembering that it is important to listen and be sensitive, it is imperative to trust your own judgement. You could be about to make a once-in-a-lifetime choice. So be wise.

There's nothing wrong with looking up to and seeking the respect of people whom you admire. As you go through life, one of the most important decisions you'll have to make will be to determine whose respect you crave most strongly. When you've made your choice, and are clear on the reasons why, you can organize your life in such a way that you behave and act in a manner that this person would approve of. What you must not do is allow yourself to be concerned or influenced by the opinions of people whom you don't really know or care about.

If, in the past, you have allowed yourself to be influenced by destructive criticism or discouraging and undermining remarks, the likelihood is you'll remember that they made you feel hurt, defensive and resentful. You must avoid these negative emotions if you are to be successful. This means ignoring the derogatory comments of people who are of no concern or value to you. These people are insecure and don't know who they are; they will always be angry and resentful towards anyone who does. You know who you are, and where you're going. Don't let these people steer you off course.

# CHAPTER 10
# LEARN TO FORGIVE

The inability to forgive someone who you deem has hurt you in some way is a major source of negative emotions. This makes you more susceptible to feelings of anger, resentment, doubt, fear and jealousy. It also causes you to blame others for any difficulties, setbacks or misfortunes that befall you.

By taking responsibility for yourself and everything that happens to you, you develop a more positive outlook. You view life in a more generous and understanding way. You become more optimistic about yourself and what you're capable of achieving. In short, you become a far more contented and effective person.

It's true that we've all had things happen to us that make us feel angry whenever we recall them; but there comes a time when we must stop dwelling on these incidents and move on. Your aim must be to totally forgive everyone in your life, no matter what they may have done to you. I know this is an extremely difficult thing to do, but it is essential that you do this, otherwise you will continue to experience disappointment, despair and deprivation.

Why can't people be nicer to each other? Why must they always criticize, complain and bicker? Why can't they cooperate? Why must they always prove points or nurse grudges? Regardless of the reason, it's a game you can leave others to play. You can't make anyone else fairer or friendlier, but you can put your own best foot forward and risk being considered naïve or weak. If it breaks a deadlock and brings progress, that's a small price to pay. Even if it seemingly brings no such tangible results, it will make you feel better about yourself. You will be amazed by what a positive attitude brings.

You can't change the way people act; you can change the way you respond. You can't control a certain situation; you can, though, adjust your attitude towards it. Don't allow anything or anyone to make you feel uncomfortable. Set about making yourself as relaxed as you can, regardless of the circumstances; then watch how things magically begin to change. Rather than wish for powers you may never get, use the many powers that you already have.

With just one word we can change a person's life. We can offer criticism that deflates, or encouragement that inspires. We can be positive or negative, resentful or forgiving, kind or callous. We don't need to say much. Often, it can be done surreptitiously. Sometimes, all it takes is a telling glance. Actions, similarly, don't have to be dramatic to be effective. Don't underestimate your power and resilience. Learn to forgive, even if you can't forget. Two wrongs don't make a right. You need to let go of a past hurt and embrace a healing future. Don't allow someone or something unimportant to take up far too much of your precious time. You have bigger things to think about. Turn your attention there!

Unless you learn to let go of your grievances, you will build your life around feelings of anger and resentment. This is why it's so important that you release yourself from your anger towards people who have hurt you. Decide right now to forgive everyone who has ever harmed or mistreated you in any way. Only by forgiving these people can you truly free yourself from the hold they have over you. "I can't forgive them," you may say. "Why should I let them get away with what they did to me? They really hurt me. They don't deserve my forgiveness." Understand that this attitude is far more harmful and detrimental to you than it is to the people you resent.

If you give forgiveness to someone, even if it is doubtful they deserve it, how can this possibly benefit you? Or them? Why should you be generous? Won't that just make you a fool? Might it not also send out the wrong message? It might, but then the biggest fools in this world are those who remain doggedly hard of heart at all times. The best message you can send anyone, regardless of past wrongdoings, is that you think the best of (and want the best for) them. Feel free to be noble and big-hearted.

Some people are reluctant to forgive because they believe that, if they forgive the other person, they're letting them off the hook. They even consider it to be doing that person a favour. The truth is: when you forgive someone, you set yourself free. This doesn't mean that you have to condone their behaviour, or even like them. All it means is forgiving them so that you can get on with the rest of your life.

When you feel anger and resentment towards another person, you're allowing them to influence your emotions. Every time you think about that person, you as good as hand over control of your emotions to them. If you refuse to forgive this individual, you continue to allow them to exert their power over your emotions, thereby condemning yourself to relive the distressing episodes over and over again.

What are your enemies doing right now? If they knew you were worrying about them, they would be rubbing their hands with glee! Just as problems can become more intense when we give them more energy, some individuals thrive on attention. You don't really have any enemies; you just have people in your life who want something you don't want. Accept as much, and relax. The more you adjust your plans in response to their actions, the more powerful you make them.

It is far better to forgive and forget than to hold onto thoughts of revenge and retribution. This maxim remains true no matter how justified your cause for grievance may be. You have to protect yourself from the negative impact of your own reactions. There is something you need to let go of. You fear, though, that if you do this, you will be sending out the wrong message. You don't want someone to think they can just 'get away' with inexcusable behaviour and expect automatic forgiveness. Understand that, by the selfless act of forgiveness, it is you that's being set free, not them. You are finally releasing yourself from the shackles that have held you back and restricted you for so long. Be careful, then, about what you wish for yourself and for others; simply let the past go and move on. To create a positive future, you need a positive attitude.

You may find it hard to forgive your past tormentors, but it is vitally important that you do so. Maybe you've held a grievance for so long that it has dominated your life. Realise that the rewards you'll gain by letting go easily outweigh anything you'll achieve by harbouring thoughts of revenge or retribution. Your whole attitude will change. You will mature into a warm-hearted, friendly, proud, generous and caring person with heaps of energy, enthusiasm, self-confidence and self-esteem.

Above all else, you must learn to forgive yourself for every bad, foolish, irresponsible, reckless and spiteful thing you have ever done. Stop dwelling on yesterday's misdemeanours; they happened in the past when you were a younger and more immature person. You're a different person now, so quit torturing yourself over something that happened in the past, something you cannot change or rectify.

Bear in mind that you may have done things, or had things done to you when you were too young, naïve or unworldly to know what was happening, how to deal with the situation or how to extricate yourself from it. We've all been in uncomfortable situations like this at some point in our lives; and we've all reacted in a way that we've later come to regret, but that doesn't make us a bad person. Understand that this was not your fault. You did the best you could in the circumstances. Remember this each time you think about the situation or the people involved until all the negative feelings you associate with it are gone.

We all do things we regret. We take actions in the heat of one moment and then, in the cool of some other moment, we wonder how we could have been so thoughtless. That is unavoidable. It is the way human nature works. We can, though, choose whether to reproach ourselves about this mercilessly and unremittingly, or just try to learn from the experience and move on. You can't change the past; but you can improve the future by forgiving your own and other people's transgressions.

Do as you would be done to. Don't (as many people are prone to do) do unto others what others have done unto you! Two wrongs never make a right. Bad behaviour is never a justification for more bad behaviour. Try your best to set a standard that others can aspire to. You can't do that if you lower yourself to the same regrettable level that some individuals in your world have sunk down to. Will that make your life difficult? No. That's fulfilling your highest potential.

Wherever there is an injustice in your life, there is an opportunity to put it right. You can't make everything perfect, but you can see the difference between a distressing situation and a truly catastrophic one. Your sense of perspective is one of your greatest assets. Nurture it.

Why do you feel it necessary to nurse a grievance? Does it benefit you in any way when you remember when someone behaved badly towards you? Do you cringe at the memory and think you'd be a fool to forget it? So don't forget. But do forgive. They say: "Leopards can't change their spots." But sometimes, people really do change. Even if they don't you have to ask yourself how much point there is in clinging on to an old resentment. Will dropping it make any difference at all? Maybe not. But it could heal a hurt in you! Life is not supposed to be a battle. By continually harping back to painful incidents, you are only hurting yourself. Make a choice right now. Either choose to follow a fury, a fever or a frenzy; or step back from a brink and be merciful. Only one option will make you truly strong! Learn to forgive and move on.

If you insist on holding a grievance towards someone, you are severely damaging yourself. Your inability to forgive even one person is enough to prevent you from progressing any further in life. Don't become one of those sad people who messed up their lives by holding onto a grudge against a certain person. Concentrate on the future rather than the past. Focus on the road ahead, not on the obstacles you've encountered along the way.

They say that we can't rewrite history. This statement, though, is only partially true. You may not be able to rewrite it, but you can change your attitude to it. If you revise any story with a sufficient number of additional facts, you will draw a different conclusion about its meaning. Often, no matter how long ago an event took place, you can effectively alter the consequences that it had, simply by understanding it better. What is the big battle that you must fight? Is it really necessary? Could you be angry with someone over a conflict that you have created in your own mind? Do you really have something to prove to someone? Or are you just trying to prove a point to yourself? In which case, why don't you do it by thinking things through rationally, and thus save a great deal of unnecessary effort? Forgive yourself for your own failings; forgive others for theirs. If you want to embrace all that's good about your future, you must start by letting go of the past.

We don't know where we were before we entered this world. We don't know where we're going once we leave it. Faced with the fact that our very existence is a list of unanswered (and unanswerable) questions, how can any of our actions seem purposeful? Because we don't know we tend not to think about it. Why shouldn't we just do whatever we want? It probably doesn't matter anyway. Ah, but it does! When we treat others with respect and show compassion and sensitivity, we become a better person. Our life takes on a true meaning, we feel spiritually uplifted. Kindness is a virtue and, though it can sometimes backfire, it can also reap immense rewards.

If there are still some areas of your life where you feel aggrieved or resentful because you continue to blame someone for something he or she did or didn't do, have the strength and honesty to admit that you too are responsible, and then let go. The best way to eliminate any kind of anger is to accept responsibility. By doing this you neutralize the feeling of anger and deprive this negative, self-destructive emotion of the energy it so badly needs to survive. It is impossible to accept responsibility for a situation and be angry at the same time. The notion of blame, on which you base your feeling of anger, is negated by your decision to accept responsibility.

Painful incidents from our past have an annoying tendency to turn up uninvited. Is there any way we can rid ourselves of this unwanted intrusion into our conscious mind? Actually, no, there isn't. There's not a bone you can bury, not an issue you can shrug off, not an event you can eradicate from your mind indefinitely. Soon or later, whatever has happened will revisit you. We must learn from every experience, painful or otherwise. Everyone has suffered an injustice at some point in their lives; it's how you learn to deal with it that counts. You can either harbour thoughts of anger, resentment and bitterness, or you can forgive and move on. Bear in mind, what goes around comes around. Every action has an equal and opposite reaction. What you give out can either help or hinder you. If you give out negative energy, you'll get back an equivalent amount of pain and hardship. If you give out thoughts of forgiveness and kindness, you will get back good fortune and happiness. This is how the universal law of cause and effect works.

You have the power to simplify a situation that has grown complicated or counterproductive. You can now make a clear, conscious decision to put a part of the past behind you. You can move forward on a fresh footing. All that's needed is a willingness to forgive a situation that you resent, to stop worrying about what caused it and whether circumstances are or were fair. Whatever has happened has happened. Only once you accept this can you wisely exert an influence over what needs to happen next.

If a mistake is recognised, and if an apology is sincere, how can it be right to hold on to anger? Nobody is expecting you to be superhuman. Just be prepared to do something very right and very compassionate. Whether they're contrite and regretful or stubborn and unrepentant, from this moment onwards forgive everyone you feel has wronged you in any way. In doing so, the negative emotions associated with the memory will fade away and eventually disappear altogether.

What causes conflict? What incites hatred? What stirs up animosity? What prevents reconciliation? These, like all big, complicated questions, have simple answers. Problems of this nature invariably have one underlying cause: intolerance. It is poisonous stuff. Indeed, intolerance is the one thing in our lives that we definitely should not tolerate! But, if we are intolerant of intolerance, we only make matters worse. What we need is patience and benevolence. No matter how justified your resentment may feel, forgiveness is the only way.

# CHAPTER 11
# SUCCESS IS A STATE OF MIND

Many of us have been exposed to negative, harmful beliefs since we were children. Being young, innocent and trusting, we unconsciously accepted these viewpoints and allowed them to play a dominant part in our lives. But, by embracing these mistaken beliefs we unintentionally did ourselves untold harm. These false beliefs would also have been accepted by our subconscious mind, which, as I have previously stated, always attempts to bring whatever we accept to fruition.

Your subconscious mind accepts whatever you impress upon it. Therefore, if you mistakenly believe something is true, your subconscious mind will also regard it as true and respond according to the nature of the suggestion. Your subconscious mind accepts every suggestion you give it, regardless of whether it is true or false.

It isn't hard to identify what your core beliefs are. But first, you must determine what a belief is. A belief is something that you assume to be true, certain and undeniable. It is usually the result of opinions, suggestions or standpoints that people impressed upon you in the past, people who you considered to be important and knowledgeable.

Now that you are aware of how the majority of your limiting beliefs originated you can begin the process of altering the impressions that were made on you in the past. The first step is to be aware of the negative opinions and attitudes that have dominated your life. Unaltered they can lead to unhappiness, anger, frustration and resentment, making the realization of your dream virtually impossible.

The next step is to realise that an opinion or suggestion cannot become rooted in your subconscious mind unless it is initially deemed to be true by your conscious mind. Your conscious mind can choose to reject any erroneous suggestions.

As you know, your subconscious mind does not make judgements or assessments, nor does it reason, conclude or work things out; that is primarily the function of your conscious mind. Your subconscious mind merely responds to the information given to it by your conscious mind. It simply accepts whatever you impress upon it. If you give it mistaken information, it will still consider it to be reliable and do its utmost to bring your suggestions (even the improbable ones) to completion as either circumstances, experiences or incidents.

A suggestion itself has no power; it can only influence you if you choose to accept it as true. Once it has been embraced by you, it becomes a belief and your subconscious will begin to react accordingly.

Here are some common limiting beliefs:

- I can't.
- No matter how hard I try, I'll still fail.
- I'll never amount to anything.
- I don't stand a chance.
- If you knew what I was really like, you wouldn't feel the same way about me.
- I haven't got a clue what to do.
- I'm always wrong.
- What's the point?
- I annoy people.

- I won't get my hopes up, I'll only be disappointed.
- I'll never get the hang of it.
- I'm bound to fail.
- It's not what you know, it's who you know.
- Things are going from bad to worse.
- Life is a constant struggle.
- I haven't got it in me.
- I'm too old.
- It is hopeless.

If you continue to accept these negative beliefs, they will hamper your chances of fulfilling your full potential. Remember, you are able to make choices. You can substitute these negative beliefs with constructive, life-enhancing affirmations whenever you want. From now on, become aware of any detrimental beliefs, opinions or suggestions that are being conveyed to you. Fill your subconscious mind with positive, enriching thoughts and you will eradicate the negative impressions that can do you so much harm.

If you carefully analyse the negative suggestions that others make to you, you will observe that many of them are made with the intention of getting you to conform to their way of thinking. Ways that are to their advantage, but not necessarily to yours.

Likewise, when you affirm to yourself that "I can't do that", "I don't stand a chance", "I'm bound to fail", "I haven't got it in me", "I'm too old", you are impressing these negative thoughts upon your subconscious. Thus you are essentially impeding your own progress.

No thoughts, whether they be positive or negative, can enter your subconscious mind without first having been accepted as true by your conscious mind. Every thought, opinion and suggestion is firstly impressed upon your conscious mind, and may either be accepted or rejected. If you choose to reject a certain idea or point of view, it will not enter your subconscious. You have absolute control over the information that reaches your subconscious mind.

You are continually being bombarded by all manner of opinions, suggestions, suppositions, propositions and notions, which are entering your subconscious mind without your knowledge. Some of these thoughts will be positive, and some negative. Now that you are aware of how damaging negative thoughts can be, you should attempt to protect your subconscious mind from any false or harmful impressions. One of your greatest gifts is your ability to choose. Choose happiness, wealth and success.

Your subconscious mind never stops working for you, not even while you sleep. You can become aware of how powerful your subconscious is by simply asking it to help you resolve a specific problem. The best time to do this is last thing at night, just before you go to sleep, the reason being that, when you become sleepy or drowsy, the conscious mind is more submissive, compliant and receptive to suggestions. When you are in this state, the negative and cynical thoughts which normally obstruct the working of your subconscious tend to subside. Therefore, your subconscious is more open to suggestions just prior to sleep or immediately upon awakening.

Your subconscious guides you by way of intuition, inklings, insights, inspiration, hints, hunches, urges, and mental images. It knows exactly where you are in relation to the end result you are aiming for.

Can you rely on your instincts? Intellectuals would say "No!" They would argue that the brain can solve all problems through logic and reason, and those that are solved any other way are the result of coincidence. Thankfully, I do not consider myself an intellectual, so I would contend that coincidence is no more than a chance occurrence and therefore cannot be relied upon. But what I do know is, if you are hearing a whisper of advice from within, it would be wise to heed it. Don't try to explain it. Just trust it.

Our brains are imperfect, inefficient and inept. Our instincts are infallible, impeccable and incomparable. Our hearts know the answers to questions before the questions have even been asked. Nor are they ever wrong, even if our powers of logic and analysis conclude that they must be. When you seek guidance from within, where a way forward needs to be found, it will be found. You may think you are struggling to make a decision. Not so. The decision has already been made. You are just struggling to justify it. Stop struggling. Just accept.

Why shouldn't we take full advantage of the intelligence we were born with? Why shouldn't we make full use of such a valuable faculty? Answer: because there will be times when the most intelligent thing we can do is ignore our own intelligence. Sometimes a little less thought and a little more passion is all that is needed to solve a vexing problem. Try using emotion and intuition, rather than logic and reasoning the next time you come up against a seeming insurmountable obstacle. When we allow our feelings an equal say, they give us shrewd guidance. Now and again, letting your heart rule your head can be the best course of action.

We are all born with natural powers that we find hard to understand or rationalize. We all know, in our heart of hearts, that we have a sixth sense available to us, which, although it may often seem to be erratic, and can frustratingly abandon us at inopportune times, is very real when it works. Don't mistakenly assume that you lack such mystical gifts. You have them. And if you trust and use them, you can make many magical changes take place.

What are your dominant thoughts? Are they positive and constructive? Or are they negative and destructive? You must ensure that they are conducive to your success and drive you towards your goal. Once you recognise that you are a self-made person, both in terms of what you do or do not achieve, and that your success or failure is determined by your habitual thinking, you'll realise that your destiny is entirely in your hands.

Where do your true talents lie? And what particular topics or tasks do you feel unqualified to cope with? You may feel that you have no talents, or that you're only capable of dealing with mundane tasks. That is complete nonsense. You are wrong to think that there's something you can't deal with or understand. Deep down you know you have what it takes. Though you may have to struggle and concentrate in order to overcome this obstacle, you can be perfectly competent when you really try. Let today be the day that brings you more confidence, makes you more aware of your true potential and shows you how to tackle difficult situations.

Now is not the time to be negative, contemptuous or dismissive about the notion of inner guidance. Nor is it the time to sit around pondering why some things may or may not be possible. It is, however, the time to realise that your life does not have to conform to someone else's understanding of reality. What is reality anyway? A 'reality' is just an illusion that everyone happens to accept and believe in. Whether you choose to conform to these indoctrinated beliefs or not is entirely up to you. Often, our opinions can be swayed by 'conventional wisdom'. Most of history's great achievements and innovations have been accomplished by those who dared to challenge and defy the accepted thinking of the time. So, don't be afraid to question long-standing, established beliefs. You are a free spirit! Indeed, if you are suffering at the moment, you are almost certainly doing so unnecessarily. Don't just 'put up' with something that's causing you distress. Remember that you are a unique individual who's entitled to enjoyment and fulfilment. If you act as if you expect it, you'll get it.

You begin the process of releasing your potential and accomplishing even greater things by challenging the beliefs that restrict and suppress your progress. These beliefs can cause you to feel inadequate, incapable or inferior in specific areas of your life. Even though these beliefs are rarely true, if you accept them as accurate assessments of your ability, you consider them to be so.

You liberate yourself from restricting beliefs by affirming to yourself that they are completely false. Then you visualize having no limitations whatsoever on your abilities. See yourself in your mind's eye having, being and doing anything you want. Imagine that your potential is unrestricted and unwavering. Picture yourself living in a bigger house, driving your dream car, or experiencing a more extravagant lifestyle. Simply see yourself living life to the full. Think of yourself as being relaxed, confident, decisive and undaunted by anything. Envisage being able to accomplish any goal you set yourself.

If you were only willing to stretch your imagination a little further, you may see a way to turn what now seems like an impossible dream into a tangible reality. At least allow yourself to consider the options you might take if only you lived in an 'ideal world'. You may yet discover that your world is more ideal than you think.

Think of something that pleases you. Now, think of something that makes you uneasy. What is the connection between these two images? Your feelings of anxiety and apprehension could be linked to a notion that good things seldom live up to your expectations; they often turn out bad. Be conscious of the fact that the positive factors in your life are far more important and powerful than any possible negative development. Don't be unnerved if things seem to be happening in the wrong order. Fundamentally, this is happening for a reason. Have more faith as you try to make sense out of a chaotic situation. You lack nothing; other, perhaps, than a sense of perspective.

We all want to feel as though we are in the right place at the right time. Sometimes, life briefly gives us that wonderful, memorable experience; but why, when it seems so natural and so right, does it prove so hard to sustain? One reason is because we doubt ourselves. We start to suspect that things are not as right as we thought they were, and those very misgivings begin to increase the suspicion that something is wrong. So much remains unknown. So much rests on circumstances beyond your control. So much has the potential to go wrong. But it could also turn out remarkably well. When an opportunity arises cherish it, don't question it. When life offers you a rare, special gift, put it to good use. Be the best you can be and life will give you the best it has to offer.

The better the way you think, the better the way you live. Every internal thought and image triggers feelings, attitudes and behaviour; they even affect the way other people react and behave towards you. Therefore, a positive self-image is essential if you are to change your life for the better.

When you absolutely accept that you are a thoroughly good, decent, hardworking, honest and intelligent person, you will exhibit this in every facet of your life. Ultimately, you will come to accept that you are an excellent person and that great success and happiness is destined for you.

# CHAPTER 12
# WHAT DO YOU BELIEVE?

People do not act in accordance with what they can achieve, but rather what they think they're capable of achieving. Therefore, if you change the way you think, you'll also change the way you act. Your self-image is formed by the mental picture you have of yourself. The way you behave, feel and react to the world around you will be consistent with the way you view yourself and your abilities. You will always act and conform to this mental image because it's the person you think you are.

To gain control over your own destiny you must be aware of the way you think, the way you perceive your surroundings and the way you relate to people. Others can foist their opinions and beliefs on you; they can either flatter you, or mock you. But whether you choose to accept these opinions or not is entirely up to you. Other people's beliefs will not become your beliefs unless you decide to accept them. Bear in mind, others can give you their opinions about you; but all that really counts is what you think about you.

If you are to fulfil your full potential it is essential that you curb your limited thinking, otherwise these negative beliefs will hinder your progress. Stop worrying about the likelihood of failure; simply concentrate on the wealth and success you could attain. You must learn to unearth, improve and appreciate the many talents that you've been blessed with.

Perhaps you should consider what you are currently going through to be a test. You have a big ambition, a precious plan. Your efforts to pursue this may, thus far, have met with encouraging results. Maybe now you are beginning to think twice. You have to ask yourself how willing you are to carry on if it isn't so simple. You may be starting to doubt the wisdom of an idea. Or maybe you're just not sure who you are and what you want any more. This is all a natural side effect of the challenging and exciting path you are heading along. You are not 'on your own', but you are isolated in one sense. This is one burden that cannot be shared, even with those who are closest to you. It may be weighing you down, yet you have to keep it aloft. You can, though, detach yourself from it just long enough for sufficient light to dawn before you start on the next stage of your journey. Such a way involves making a conscious effort not to feel anxious or concerned about how things will turn out. Trust more, and make better use of the facilities and options that are open to you. Be truly resourceful now. Give yourself a pep talk, and then commit to seeing your plan through to completion.

People rarely become wise overnight. Usually, our most valuable insights take time to develop. We have days on which it seems as if these ideas have suddenly sprung forth from out of nowhere, but, in reality, such moments are usually the result of a long process of contemplation. Until the moment when a subconscious impulse becomes a vivid recognition, we can only wait and wonder. Once there's real understanding, though, why should there be any further delay? There's always the slight danger of acting too hastily, but all will be well as long as you hold off just long enough for sufficient light to dawn before forging ahead.

Aim to become so self-assured, daring, powerful, fearless and determined that you can set yourself any goal with the certain knowledge that you'll eventually achieve it. Once you reach this heightened state, your resolve will be so strong that you'll allow nothing or nobody to come between you and your ultimate goal.

When you examine your core beliefs regularly, you can see where you might be deceiving yourself or discounting information that could be to your advantage. Many people block out the truth because they don't want to be proved wrong, feel deluded or look stupid. Negative beliefs or opinions are often formed on the basis of a false assumption. As is often the case, discovering one single new fact about someone or something can completely change our attitude towards him, her or it.

When you're absolutely convinced that what you believe is true, you remain steadfast in your beliefs and totally reject any conflicting opinions. It is impossible to hold opposing beliefs in your mind without feeling anxious, insecure and vulnerable. So, in order to prove that you are right, you search frantically for any information, facts or statistics that support your beliefs. But by doing this you are disregarding information that could be beneficial to you; because you are viewing the truth as you see it, not how it actually is. For this reason you must constantly examine your principal beliefs, otherwise you may continue to hold onto thoughts, opinions and attitudes that can sabotage your entire life.

None of us is infallible; but that's nothing to be ashamed of. Only fools think they know it all. Wise, capable people have a more level-headed self-image. They acknowledge their own limitations, encourage themselves to go beyond these and yet feel willing, if necessary, to concede the occasional defeat. They've come to realise that, as long as they persevere, they will eventually turn a bad situation around. They have confidence, but they do not let it turn into arrogance. The doubt that you may now feel is not a reason to give up. It is a reason to proceed with caution. The disappointments you have suffered are merely hurdles that, if you keep trying, you can easily jump!

Sometimes, things work out wonderfully. Arrangements fall into place. Convenient coincidences crop up. We feel as if we are 'in the flow' and can't put a foot wrong. Then there are times when the opposite occurs. Nothing fits. Everything fails. We get sucked into a black hole of despair, from which we can see no way out. We feel like throwing in the towel. Yet both conditions are, in reality, two sides of one coin. Almost all things can be put right with patience, faith and understanding. If you persevere, you can turn a situation right round.

One day you'll look back on your difficult experiences and feel less inclined to blame yourself for problems or to feel you have been somehow punished for making 'mistakes'. Yet for as long as you are willing to shoulder responsibility for circumstances that have been beyond your control, others will let you labour under that misconception. It suits them to do so.

Those of us with sensitive souls must be wary of over-exposure to those with harder hearts. You can put up a good pretence of being tough and indifferent, but deep down you feel aggrieved each time you encounter someone who is unkind, unfair or contemptuous. Your ideals are far too precious to be compromised. Seek out people who will encourage and motivate you. Ignore those who try to undermine you.

We all have people we respect and admire. But this can have its drawbacks. When we put anyone on a pedestal or hold them in overly high esteem, we rob ourselves of something. Instead of looking within ourselves and expecting some wonderful characteristic to emerge, we make an irrational comparison and, unsurprisingly, find ourselves wanting. The only standards you must live up to are your own. We all want someone or something to look up to. We need to feel that we belong. We need to feel that our life has purpose. We need to feel wanted. We also need to feel that we are connected to some higher intelligence that will steer us in the right direction. Sometimes, this need causes us to abdicate responsibility for our own actions and choices. You are clouding your judgement when you allow a sense of need to overwhelm you. You are more likely to get the right result if you can only persuade yourself that you know what's best for you. Grant yourself permission to be yourself and to trust yourself. Perspective and perseverance are the keys that can open every locked door.

We give some people too much power over us. We allow them to find where our weaknesses are and, in so doing, invite them to exploit these frailties. We permit some situations to matter more than they really ought to. Why? Because we need to experience vulnerability from time to time. If we simply swagger around acting cool, calm, confident and controlled, we end up looking shallow and lose our credibility. There is, though, a point beyond which we should not go. Pull back from that brink and reclaim your power.

Almost everything we say or do is either to increase our self-esteem or defend ourselves against those who seek to belittle or demean us. If you lack confidence you will be easily affected by the way that other people behave towards you. You will have a tendency to take everything personally; as if the whole world were somehow conspiring against you. If someone doesn't treat you with the respect you think you deserve, you will take it as a personal affront; whereas, it's often the case that the person in question is so preoccupied with his own problems that he's totally oblivious to his insensitive behaviour. That's why it's so silly to get angry over someone's thoughtless actions.

An effective way of neutralizing negative thoughts is to exert control over your emotions and behaviour by firmly resolving not to dwell on any negative feelings you may have about unfortunate, regrettable, distressing or annoying situations that are bound to occur. Simply stop exhibiting signs of anger, irritability, disappointment, frustration or resentment, either to yourself or those around you.

Some people say it's good to show your feelings. But what they don't realise is that by doing so you are actually exacerbating the situation, because whatever you focus on and draw attention to becomes your reality. If a small, negative emotion is not nipped in the bud, it can spread like wildfire and before long grow into something that dominates your thoughts.

How do you turn a small problem into a major catastrophe? You just let your emotions get the better of you. You vent your rage, say what you secretly think, or do what you know you ought not to. Resist the temptation to express your anger because everything will automatically go from bad to worse the moment you start giving way to your negative emotions. And is the reverse true? Can you really turn a big problem into an inconsequential matter just by rising above it? Yes. Try it and see for yourself. For though there may be some genuine reasons to feel disgruntled, there are even better reasons to feel optimistic. Focus your attention on those.

You must deliberately take control of your thoughts, or they will control you. The opinions and beliefs you have about yourself cannot be totally overlooked because they are locked in your subconscious, but they can be neutralized through correct thinking. This new perspective will then become your principal belief, because it is impossible to hold two conflicting viewpoints at the same time. Remember, people always act in accordance with their predominant opinions or beliefs.

You probably have deep-rooted beliefs about yourself that are holding you back. These opinions may be completely mistaken, but, if you continue to hold onto them, they will severely hinder your progress. It's never too late to change your beliefs. Too often we make excuses for ourselves. We say things like "I've always been this way", or "I can't change who I am", or "I'm too old to change my ways now". This way of thinking will get you nowhere. Never judge yourself by your past performances; instead see each and every day as a new beginning.

Is someone else having a better time than you are? If that's what you suspect, it's automatically, inevitably true. Okay. Pay close attention to this statement. Anyone, anywhere on this Earth, who isn't worried about whether someone else is doing better than they are is always going to be doing better than the person who is worrying about it! You shouldn't want to trade places with anyone. You should enjoy what you've got and give yourself wholeheartedly to what you're doing. If you must make comparisons, take a good look at those you really don't envy; and count your blessings.

Are you allowed to be happy? Will something go horribly wrong if you start to enjoy a situation that seems to be turning out well? Must you keep careful track of everyone and everything in case the wrong move is made? Not unless you want to end up a nervous wreck! Be careful not to let apprehension weigh you down. Provided you keep an eye on the progress (or the lack of it) within a crucial area of your life, you will be ready to take action where appropriate. You will also be able to identify the areas in which no action need be taken. More often than not, the right things will happen automatically.

Every person has a different understanding and perception of their situation. This is what makes us unique and distinct individuals. Even though we inhabit the same world and encounter the same type of people, experiences and information, we interpret them in different ways. If our perception of reality is faulty, it follows that our attitude, thoughts, opinions and actions will also be faulty.

If you're not sure whether your current situation merits a smile or a frown, or if you feel apprehensive, fearful, suspicious or troubled, you must look upon the dilemma before you as a chance to conquer a fear or lay to rest a ghost from the past. Though you may not be keen to encounter a particular problem or situation, you will benefit enormously from doing so, bravely. Try looking at your situation in the same open-minded, innocent way that a young child might. Don't categorise everything as 'good' or 'bad'. Don't prejudge the outcome of the drama that's being played out. Don't attempt to understand what's going on. Just trust that something, somewhere, has your best interests at heart. Your view of a particular matter can often be clouded. Ignore your opinions. Allow yourself an open mind. And be ready for the right kind of change.

It is the quality of your thoughts that will ultimately determine the quality of your life. Positive thinking leads to greater independence, success, happiness and peace of mind; negative thinking undermines your self-confidence and self-esteem, rendering you virtually ineffective in the vital areas of your life. You have an incredibly creative mind and an amazing capacity for success and achievement. You just need to learn how to harness this potential.

If you constantly think about failure, disappointment and regret, this will only serve to diminish your self-esteem. This type of thinking is corrosive; it will eventually lead to anger, stress, anxiety and unhappiness. Whereas, if you see yourself as a positive person, filled with talent, energy and creativity, these fundamental beliefs will drive you to set goals, work tirelessly, think constructively, brush aside setbacks and ultimately prevail.

You should adopt a more positive attitude and believe that not only are you good enough, but you have the ability and flair to excel in whatever you choose to do. You must believe that you are capable of achieving anything you set your mind on.

If you don't believe in yourself, nobody else will! You must build a positive frame of mind. Never fall into the trap of saying "I can't"; this is incredibly self-destructive. Once you start thinking negatively, you begin to lose your self-belief, and once that is lost the task ahead becomes tedious and laborious.

Avoid negative thoughts; they are dangerous, destructive and demoralizing. Instead, say to yourself "I can" and "I will". It's amazing the effects that these two statements can have. They can completely alter your state of mind; you begin to think more constructively and imaginatively. You get out of that defeated mentality and start thinking and believing positively.

Have faith in your ability and resolve never to allow negative thoughts to impede your progress. When you do this you should start feeling more secure and confident. There is less to worry about, less to fear and less to threaten you. Rejoice in the progress that you are making in key areas of your life and start looking for ways to increase and strengthen it. For, with a little effort and wisdom, you can make crucial headway by taking momentous decisions that will somehow enable you to permanently improve your position.

Once you develop the right attitude, you'll realise you can do anything you truly desire. Your ability hasn't anything to do with it; it's how much you want to succeed that counts. Everyone has the ability to improve. You can, and will if you really want to.

# CHAPTER 13
# HAVE A WRITTEN PLAN

What are you dreaming of? What are you longing for? How sure do you feel that, one day, your aspiration will be fulfilled? If your hopes are anything other than high, alter them. Think positive. Think big, but be realistic. Don't expect an immediate transformation. Even so, you are entitled to expect a significant improvement in your circumstances. For now is your chance to forge ahead to a brighter tomorrow by thinking constructively and methodically, thereby bringing calm, order and enlightenment to an area of your life that has hitherto been chaotic and confused. Don't assume that everything has to stay the way it has always been. If you really want change, you can have it. By taking these first, tentative steps, you may yet set off a chain of events that, by some means or other, leads you inexorably closer to your destiny. Stay resolute and committed to your goal. Then you will stand a much better chance of actually getting it.

The most important element of dreaming big is being able to determine exactly what you want to achieve in life. You must gaze into the future and envisage having no obstructions standing between you and your desires. To keep this prospective belief alive, you must use your imagination. A sequence of future events is conjured up in your mind, or a total scenario invented. These projections into the future can have a positive effect on your results. The technique of visualization has been used to great effect to change the limited belief systems of many people. Once you have extricated yourself from the bonds of limited thinking, you can start to turn your dreams and fantasies into reachable goals.

The ability to determine your goal and develop a plan of action is the key to your success. Once you have mastered this skill, there are no limits to what you can accomplish. People who have clear, specific goals, and know exactly what they want are far more likely to succeed than those who simply hope for the best. Setting goals can be difficult, but it is essential if you are to prevail. With clear goals you can achieve almost anything; without them you'll struggle all the way.

When you set a clear goal for yourself, and know exactly where you want to go, you'll eventually get into the habit of doing only those things that move you closer to your goal. You will use your time far more productively, on things that propel you forward. You'll have neither the time nor the inclination to waste your energy on activities that are not beneficial to you.

The reason why many people fail to achieve their goal is because they've wasted so much time doing things of little or no value to themselves. And the reason for this time wasting is a lack of vision and purpose. They have no idea what they want. If you are to be successful, you must know exactly what it is that you want to achieve. You must picture your goals with as much clarity and detail as you can muster. Visualize your aspirations as many times a day as you can; and when you do this, imagine how you would feel if you'd already accomplished this objective. The best times to do this exercise are last thing at night and first thing in the morning. The more adept you become at visualizing your goal, until it becomes a living, breathing, thrilling and vivid picture in your mind, the more resolute and purposeful you will become.

The purpose of creating a written plan that outlines your specific goals and how you aim to accomplish them is to give you something tangible to aim for. It helps to strengthen your belief and reinforce your certainty that your aims are attainable.

Clear and written goals focus your attention and concentrate your mind on the direction you intend to go, and what you want to achieve. With clear, specific goals you will accomplish a great deal more than you otherwise would have, and you will have greater vision and clarity. But the greatest benefit to goals is that they give you far more confidence and enable you to feel far more in control of events. This is because you are absolutely clear about what you are aiming for.

Setting goals is simply a matter of making decisions. It's about knowing where you want to go. Put another way, if you're not sure where you are going, you will probably end up in the wrong place. If you're not achieving what you are capable of achieving, it's because you haven't clearly outlined your objectives.

Your plan should contain a detailed list of all the things you need to do to help you achieve your goal. Once you have completed your list, you can add new ideas as they spring to mind. Thinking carefully and planning thoroughly will greatly increase the likelihood of you reaching your targets.

A written plan gives you a sense of purpose and direction. It strengthens your desire and determination to succeed. When you write down what you will have to do to fulfil your desires, you're proving to yourself that you have the skills and expertise that are needed to succeed. Your written plan will give you the strength and resolve to keep going, no matter what obstacles or difficulties you may encounter along the way. It will help you to see how far you've come, and how far you have to go. It will also help you define your objectives; and whenever you refer to your plan, you will be reminded of what you want, and why you want it.

When you start working slowly and methodically towards something of great importance to yourself, you find yourself developing a strength and persistence that help you achieve things that you wouldn't have previously thought possible.

The speed at which you achieve your goals once you've committed them to paper is absolutely incredible. The act of writing out your plan crystallizes your thoughts; and thoughts provoke action. You'll also save time and energy because you will know exactly where you're going. And when obstacles are put in your way, your written plan will ensure that you overcome them and get back on track.

You won't be totally committed to achieving your goal unless you are clear about the benefits you'll enjoy. This is an extremely important and essential step towards creating the ideal end result. No matter what you are doing, if you're unsure of the prize you'll gain by doing it, maintaining the necessary level of enthusiasm will be extremely difficult. When you're unsure of the benefits, it always makes whatever you're doing seem far more demanding and laborious.

You'll be unable to fully commit yourself towards the accomplishment of anything unless you can identify the reward you'll gain from the efforts you expend. If you are clear about the benefits, you will gladly pay the price. The main difference between those who fulfil their ambition and those who don't is desire. Rewards generate desire, so you must be clear about the benefits and rewards you'll gain.

A goal is something that must have a measurable benefit upon its completion. If your goal has no inherent reward, it cannot be defined as a goal. Outlining the benefits and rewards you'll obtain upon the achievement of your goal must be a key component of your written plan.

Your ability to draw up written goals and devise plans for their fulfilment is crucial to your success. A plan of action gives you a sense of direction. It builds up your level of belief and increases your desire. You eventually become convinced that your goal is actually attainable.

Do something every single day that moves you closer to your goal. If you are to maintain your hunger, persistence and self-belief, you must do something each day that generates a feeling of advancement and progress.

A major determinant to the success of goals is positive feedback. Therefore, it makes sense to draw up a list of the goals you've achieved. Included in this list must be the obstacles and pitfalls you've overcome to get this far. Every little success must be noted, always adding to your list of completed goals. Every time you refer to this list you will feel a sense of achievement and satisfaction; you'll know there are virtually no limits to what you can achieve.

Decide in advance that you are never going to give up on moving towards your ultimate goal, no matter what setbacks or obstacles you may encounter along the way. This is sometimes difficult, because your natural tendency will be to become discouraged, disheartened and disappointed. You might start to dwell on how hard it will be to overcome these obstacles and roadblocks. If this happens, remind yourself of the prizes you'll ultimately acquire until you feel they totally overshadow any obstacles you can foresee.

Write down your plan and take action on it immediately. Discipline yourself to do something every day that propels you towards your principal goal. This may seem like a very simple process, but it is extremely powerful and must never be underestimated. To do so would severely hinder your chances of success. Developing this habit will reward you in every area of your life.

You deserve better. But you are only going to get that if you make room for it in your life. Why settle for second best? Why cheat yourself out of an entitlement? Why not think big and be brave? You are not just watching the movie of your life like a passive viewer. You are writing the script and directing the film.

# CHAPTER 14
# CHALLENGE YOUR BELIEFS

Everybody develops a set of beliefs about themselves, starting from childhood. This self-image becomes instilled in your subconscious mind, which accepts everything you impress upon it, or what you consciously believe. Your subconscious mind is like a bed of soil: it will grow all kinds of seeds, whether they be good or bad; it makes no distinction. It will obediently accept any proposition impressed upon it. Your self-image influences and determines what you feel, say, experience and achieve. Therefore, if you want to see better results, you must change the way you perceive yourself in your mind's eye.

Every belief, opinion or value you have at this point in time, you learned as a child. What you are today is the result of beliefs or opinions you were given when you were at an impressionable age. Beliefs and opinions you accepted as being true. When you firmly believe something to be true, it is true as far as you're concerned, regardless of any evidence to the contrary.

One reason why we have poor judgement is because our minds have been manipulated from an early age. Teachers show us how we should think and act if we wish to better ourselves. But is this because they are genuinely concerned about our future wellbeing, or is it a cunning way of maintaining classroom discipline? Parents twist the truth for various domestic reasons. Then, what happens when we turn on the T.V.? Advertisement after advertisement will blatantly lie to us about what is guaranteed to make us feel happy and fulfilled. What do people really mean? Where is their hidden agenda? What is their motivation? How can we be sure they truly have our best interests at heart? You are an adult now. Think for yourself and choose wisely.

You are not powerless. You have, though, the power to perceive yourself as without power if you so choose. Tell someone this is how you feel and they may give you advice. If you take it, you will effectively be giving them power over you. Then you may end up powerless! Power is much easier to give than to take. Watch out for a tendency to create the very situation you would most like to avoid ending up in. The more you worry, the more vulnerable you become.

What do you have to be thankful for? What are you entitled to resent? Automatically, unconsciously, we make judgements about events, circumstances and experiences. We deem them good or bad and then think no further about whether we have applied the correct label. No process of selection, though, is ever perfect. We all mistakenly celebrate gains of dubious merit. We all complain about factors we should be glad of. Look again at something that seems to be a problem. Actually, it's a gift. Accept it, embrace it and watch everything improve as a direct result of your new, wise understanding.

The greater the number of people who feel sure of something, the harder it becomes to question it. But if you are the only person who holds a particular opinion, you can expect to be thought of as a maverick, regardless of how accurate and decisive your ideas may actually be. In this regard, at least, there is not just safety in numbers, but great danger in them, too. You find yourself defending what would seem to be a minority point of view. That doesn't mean, though, that your beliefs are unfounded.

People say all kinds of things. They utter complete garbage. They air their prejudices. They bombard you with unsubstantiated claims, assertions and assumptions. Yet they make these statements in a manner that implies unquestionable authority. We listen to them, take their statements seriously, and end up letting ourselves be unduly influenced by their ideas and beliefs. You can't allow yourself to be led this way any longer. You've got to stick with what you're sure of. And, if you're not sure what you're sure of, allow yourself to remain unsure! It's far wiser to remain in confusion than linger in delusion!

It's not what you experience in life that's important; it's how you react to these experiences. How you react to people and events is determined by your fundamental beliefs. These are the thoughts, ideas, opinions and principles you have accumulated throughout your life. For instance, you may have feelings of inferiority or insecurity. You think that people who have achieved more than you are better than you. You assume that they must be superior to you; so it must logically follow that you are inferior to them.

Some people are better educated than others. They have attended more classes, passed more exams. Does this mean they are more knowledgeable? Only in a limited, superficial way. We are all born blessed with equal access to a universal library full of profound insight and important information. To consult it, we don't have to train our brains, we simply have to hear our hearts. Just as a salmon instinctively knows its way to the spawning ground, your intuition knows the right answer.

You may have reservations about taking on a new challenge. You may be of the opinion that you are playing out a familiar drama and there's not much chance of it having a different outcome. But you can't be so sure of that. Indeed, you can't be sure of much at all. That is what is so exciting and potentially beneficial about your situation. There is a big unknown and it is every bit as likely to work in your favour as it is to work against you. Be open-minded and you will start to feel far better.

You are not as restricted as you fear. You can see reasons to worry. You possibly feel it is most unwise to ignore such indications. But in allowing them to dominate your thoughts, you are giving them more power than they deserve. There is something you want. You are entitled to want this. Indeed, you are entitled not just to want it, but to find a way to get it. Don't stand in your own way. Don't be beaten by pessimism.

You are a unique individual who has something exceptional to offer. Others may be a bit like you, but nobody is exactly like you. You can, if you choose, make a significant contribution. But while you mustn't develop an inflated notion of your own importance, you shouldn't feel insignificant either. You can make a difference.

One weakness that many of us suffer from is a tendency to undervalue our own strengths. We do ourselves down. We doubt our own abilities. We always go for the safe option, the one that isn't too challenging. Yet it is only through stretching ourselves a little that we ever reach our full potential. Go one step at a time. If you reach a point where you're stuck, change direction. The likelihood is, though, that you'll keep making progress. The obstacles in your path will prove easy enough to overcome. It's the ones in your mind that are going to prove trickier. These are theoretical, emotional, imaginary and based on fear. Practical solutions don't drive them away. Only inspired ideas and heartfelt expressions defeat them. The more you think about a problem the bigger you'll make it. The more you just get on with what needs to be done, the greater your chance of success.

You are strong, important and powerful. The fact that you are not getting quite what you think you want from life does not alter this. Even the most influential and successful people find themselves falling flat on their face now and again. Don't misjudge your situation. You are not, by any stretch of the imagination, on your face; you are merely teetering slightly. Steady yourself and seek guidance. You will be given a revelation. You'll see how secure your future actually is.

# CHAPTER 15
# WHO ARE YOU?

Who are you? By this, I don't mean who are you pretending to be. Nor who you think you ought to be, or who you have been at various points in your life. The question is: who are you really? What are you truly capable of? What makes you unique? What great potential lies trapped inside you? What hidden treasures remain undiscovered? If you constantly ask yourself these questions, you'll eventually get an answer that changes everything.

Do you know who you are? Or do you just know who you're trying to be? There's a subtle but key difference. Often in our lives, we blur the boundary between our true selves and the character we feel obliged to play to maintain our credibility. When we lose touch with ourselves, all our relationships suffer, as do our chances of advancing. All our energy is directed towards maintaining this elaborate charade to the point where almost everything else takes second place. Many regrettable instances in our lives can be linked to a fear of honesty. There's no reason to fear that.

Do you want to become a different person? Do you want to start leading another life? It is tempting, when we are under duress, to start entertaining radical aspirations. Our yearning for change grows more intense as it becomes apparent that, the way they are, things aren't good. But really you don't need a big transformation. You only need a small, crucial factor to alter. Fix that by being honest with yourself about what you want. Bear in mind, there is one thing you are exceptionally good at. You are truly magnificent at the art of 'being yourself'. Nobody else can match you in that regard. It just so happens that, if you wish to see a marked improvement in your circumstances, this is the only thing you need do, or be.

"Knowledge of the self is the mother of all knowledge." So said the poet Kahlil Gibran. This may well be the case. But how can we be sure? Few of us know ourselves well enough to know whether we really know ourselves at all. How well do you know yourself? A process of inner discovery may be all that's needed to help you gain a new, more enlightened perspective. Seek silence and solitude occasionally. Allow your mind to drift. Then see what ideas and innovations surface from your inner depths. Don't dismiss the notion that emerges just because it doesn't seem to make sense. Your receiving a gift; a helpful clue, an inspired insight. Trust it. Explore it. But, most importantly, act on it! The power of the mind knows no bounds. You can harness this power by relaxing, thinking positive thoughts and by letting an inner vision of confidence shine through. You'll be amazed at the effect this has. It can often result in a complete reversal of fortune.

To take full control of your life, it's important that you know exactly who you are. Your self-image, which is how you see yourself in your mind, determines everything you say, do and think. You literally act, feel and behave according to this mental image. You will always act in a manner that's consistent with the way you see yourself.

Whether you're aware of it or not, you created and sculpted the person that you are today. The way you walk, the way you talk, what you think and believe have all been learned, imitated, instilled or acquired. Every characteristic, habit, peculiarity and mannerism has been copied and borrowed from somebody. It may have been a member of your family, a friend, a character in a book, a celebrity or a movie star. We all tend to copy people we admire.

Just because you've formed your personality by imitating others, this doesn't mean you're a fraud. Draw some comfort from the fact that nobody else will have combined the exact same characteristics, mannerisms and traits that you have. Nor does it mean that you're not a unique individual. The great advantage to this is that, since you assembled your personality from scratch, you can alter it any time you choose. It's not the end of the world when you discover that you're not the person you always thought you were. On the contrary, it's the first day of your new and improved life.

Your self-image is made up of all your beliefs about yourself and your capabilities. This set of beliefs includes all the emotions, experiences, ideas, opinions, knowledge, decisions, successes and failures you've accumulated up till now. They influence how you feel about yourself and how well you think you're doing overall. Your self-image determines how you think, feel, react and function in every area of your life that you consider important.

You may have formed your self-image on the basis of totally flawed information, or through mistaken or distorted beliefs that you've adopted. Even so, once you hold these beliefs, you do not question their authenticity. You'd probably be hard-pressed to remember how, when or why you formed these beliefs; you just live your life as though they're true. Even if they're not true, you believe they are. These beliefs are based mostly on information you've absorbed, accepted and embraced, regardless of any evidence or proof.

No two people's fingerprints are the same. Our DNA connects us to our family, but it also marks us apart as unique. Even identical twins born within seconds of each other will have different and distinct personalities. Why, then, do we measure ourselves by the points we seemingly have in common with those around us? What is possible for someone else may be impossible for you and, crucially, the reverse is true. Your life may be superficially similar to someone else's. The two of you may have many experiences in common and there may be many feelings you share. Still, be careful about making a comparison. You are different people with different needs and motivations. You can't expect something to happen to you just because it has happened to someone else. A colleague may have run into trouble through pursuing a certain goal, but it could prove very successful for you.

Many questions need to be asked. To each of these, there's an answer somewhere, waiting to be found. In every case, that answer involves a piece of information you can profit from, albeit subtly in some instances. Don't be afraid of what you may find out. You are not opening a can of worms or taking the lid off Pandora's Box. You are equipping yourself with knowledge, and you know what they say about knowledge. It is power. How can you operate effectively if you're stumbling in the dark? Take your opportunity to switch on the light and then endeavour to overcome whatever obstacle has been holding you back for too long.

What happens when you turn the light on in a dark room? Nothing actually changes; it's just that suddenly you see what before you could only imagine. Gloomy shadows disappear. Clear, clean lines emerge. It's amazing how a little extra information can alter a perception. Admittedly, it can also reveal faults and failings that were previously indiscernible. Ultimately, though, it is better to be fully informed than to live in ignorance.

Beliefs that restrict you in any way are the worst of all. They can cause you to feel inadequate or lacking in a specific area. These beliefs are hardly ever accurate, but if you accept them as a sound assessment of your ability, they become true for you. You must recognize that your mind is playing tricks on you. This is not the truth about you.

For you to fulfil your potential and pursue your passions, you must challenge your beliefs. In order to rid yourself of these restricting beliefs, you must regard them as completely false; then affirm to yourself how you're going to succeed in your goal. Shut out all negative thoughts. See yourself performing to your full ability. Your self-image controls how you perform; it cannot act contrary to the thoughts you are holding. Expect and anticipate the best for yourself. Once you fix in your mind a preconceived notion of how you think things are going to work out, you invariably go on to create that situation or conjure up the circumstances to make it happen. So, your self-image can either reinforce an existing belief or alter the opinion you have about yourself; thereby altering the end result.

You can easily look at what's happening in your life now and decide it ought to be very different. Or, you can look at the same sequence of events and decide that they are perfect, just as they are. What does this tell you? It tells you that opinions and expectations are vital. That's good. After all, it is usually much easier to alter an attitude than to change a situation. Reach within for strength, insight, guidance and inspiration. What you believe to be true will turn out to be true. So believe only good things.

If you change one thing, will everything else change too? Not necessarily. It depends not so much on what you are trying to change, but why. Don't see every factor in your life as being somehow connected to every other factor. You can easily make adjustments without creating further ramifications. Unless, that is, you are kidding yourself. Perhaps, secretly, deep within, you want to change everything. You can make that happen, too. But only if that is what you choose.

You have a special friend. There is someone who cares deeply about you and wants the best for you. Who is this person who will do anything they can to help you? Go find a mirror. Look into it. Smile at yourself. You have become too critical, doubtful, fearful and judgemental. What's more, you have become disengaged, distant and detached. Worst of all, you have lost sight of your importance, value and uniqueness. It's about time you got to know and appreciate the real you. Do that, and all other factors will soon improve.

If you're not entirely sure you know who you are any more, remember who you used to be. Then ask yourself who you'd like to become. This will help you gauge your current position. See yourself as someone who is on the way from where they used to be to where they intend to go. Therefore you must be in the right place, for the time being at least. And people who are in 'the right place' find that the right things happen naturally around them. New opportunities arise. Obstacles hitherto deemed insurmountable suddenly seem far less daunting. You feel enthusiastic, passionate and confident about what you're doing. Life becomes more carefree and enjoyable; it is no longer a struggle and a headache. This is no time to be giving up hope. If you're ready for magic to enter your life, it will yet find a way.

# CHAPTER 16
# BE OPTIMISTIC

One of the most potent qualities for success is optimism. Optimistic people believe they can achieve great things and are continually striving to do just that. They look for the positive in every situation; and when something does go wrong, they find something good to take from that problem or setback and look upon it as a learning and growing experience. If any problem crops up, far from fearing or avoiding it, they see it as an enticing challenge and resolve to tackle it. They have no concerns about taking risks, which is why they are invariably so successful. They don't fear failure because, as they see it, failures are inevitable stepping stones on the road to success. If you can view each setback as a learning experience that will eventually lead you to certain success, you will become far more effective and achieve all of your goals.

How you respond to the inevitable problems that will arise will be a true test of your resilience. Life can at times be a constant succession of problems and troublesome situations. When these occur, you should stay calm, take stock of the situation and immediately begin a plan of action to remedy the situation. If you're able to stay focused, you will usually find the best course of action to take.

A positive attitude and an optimistic outlook towards yourself and your goals are essential if you are to grow. This, together with total self-confidence, is what is needed if you are to fulfil your ambitions. Once you set yourself a goal, your attitude can either help or hinder your chances of success. The attitudes you have formed compel you to either pursue certain situations or avoid them completely.

Attitudes themselves are neither positive nor negative, but they are an indication of your predominant feelings. You've probably picked most of them up unintentionally, without even realizing it. Even so, they're largely responsible for the feelings, thoughts, behaviour and actions that govern every aspect of your life.

If you develop a positive and constructive self-image, this will cause you to do things that make you come out on top. Losing will not be an option for you. This is why having the right attitude is so important; it determines the difference between success and failure.

So, to be successful you must set yourself higher goals, and know how you are going to achieve them. You should draw-up a detailed step-by-step plan of what you need to do to achieve what you desire. Remember, you're in charge. If you don't like what's happening in your life, then you should change it for the better, and do it right now.

To be successful you should set yourself clear and specific targets for what you want to achieve, and then work out meticulously how you intend to see these through to completion. Think carefully about what you must do, and when you have made up your mind, act decisively.

Once you have a clear plan of what you must do to achieve success, you will feel far more relaxed and confident. You will definitely know which path your life is taking; the path that leads to success and happiness.

You must set high standards for yourself, and always strive to meet these standards or, better still, surpass them. You should be extremely ambitious, and always believe you are capable of even greater things. You will be surprised at the effect that this positive outlook has on your overall performance.

A positive mental attitude is essential if you are to be successful in any venture. There are bound to be some setbacks and disappointments along the way; but you should remain strong, resilient and optimistic so as to bounce back from these inevitable occurrences. A positive mental attitude is the characteristic of a winner, and this is what will ensure your success.

You must decide where you want to be a few years from now, and how you are going to get from where you are now to where you want to be. When you're sure about where you are coming from and where you want to go, you become far more effective at realistically planning for the future.

Clear and written goals focus your attention and concentrate your mind on the direction you intend to go, and on what you want to achieve. With clear, specific goals you will accomplish a great deal more than you otherwise would have, and you will have greater vision and clarity. But the greatest benefit to goals is that they give you a sense of direction and enable you to feel far more in control of events. This is because you are absolutely clear about what you want to achieve. When you start working slowly and methodically towards something of great importance to yourself, you find that you develop a strength and persistence that helps you accomplish things you wouldn't have previously thought possible.

If you don't believe in yourself, nobody else will! You must build a positive frame of mind. Never fall into the trap of saying "I can't"; this is incredibly self-destructive. Once you start thinking negatively, you begin to lose your self-belief, which is a vital weapon in your armoury.

Avoid negative thoughts; they are dangerous, destructive and corrosive. Instead, say to yourself "I can" and "I will". It's amazing the effect that these two statements can have. They can completely alter your state of mind; you begin to think more positively and imaginatively, and ultimately discover that, in fact, you actually can.

By setting yourself realistic targets and planning meticulously to meet these targets, you will be moving inexorably towards your most important goal. To maintain this momentum you must do something every single day that gives you a feeling of making progress. This will help you generate a sense of confidence and enthusiasm, and give you a chance to believe in yourself.

Your desire to reach your goal must be so strong that it will spur you on, through both the good times and the bad, the fears and the doubts, and the problems and the setbacks. Be absolutely clear about what you want to achieve; this is essential if you are to succeed.

Always set yourself the highest standards in every aspect of your life, and then be tenacious in your efforts to meet these standards. Remember, you will never get any more out of your venture than you put into it. But what you put in you will definitely get back, and more besides.

When you develop the right attitude you can do anything you really desire. Your ability hasn't anything to do with it; it's how much you want to succeed that counts. Everyone has the ability to improve. You can, and will if you really want to.

Eliminate the fear of failure. Failure is a condition which is common to most people. We are conditioned into believing that failure is the most terrible thing that can happen to us. You must develop the habit of thinking that every failure brings you a little bit closer to the success you crave. Look upon each failure as a minor setback that you can learn lessons from. Almost every high achiever has had many failures along the way; but they persevered until success finally came. Always bear in mind that there can be no success without the inevitable and unavoidable failure. Whether or not you're capable of dealing with these problems will be a crucial factor in determining how far you progress. Remember, you haven't failed at anything until you actually give up.

When things are going well, life is great. It's when things aren't doing quite so well that a person must remain optimistic and draw upon all his or her resources to get back on track. So, always think positively and constructively. Constantly reaffirm to yourself "I can" and "I will".

**NEGATIVE THOUGHTS ARE EXTREMELY CORROSIVE—AVOID THEM AT ALL COSTS.**

Always think of yourself as a winner; failure can never triumph over persistence. If you learn to conquer your fear of failure, success will come eventually. That's guaranteed!

Keep on going! Remember, you haven't failed until you say to yourself "I give up!" Failures count for absolutely nothing if you succeed in the end.

# CHAPTER 17
# HOW TO COMBAT STRESS

Stress is a complex condition of body and mind caused by unusual, distressing or threatening situations in our external world. The condition may be short- or long-term, and the causes may be predominantly either physiological or psychological, with the latter tending to be the more troublesome. All human beings, from birth to death, are subject to periods of stress. This is because we live in a dangerous and hostile world in which the unexpected is always likely to occur.

Short-term stress is the kind of situation which arises when we are briefly startled or shocked by something, such as a loud noise, a sudden movement or a sharp pain. These unnerving incidents are mostly short-lived because corrective action is easily taken, generally automatically, by our body's natural defence mechanisms. Occasionally these stressful occurrences may not be physically based. For example, you may be shocked or upset by an unpleasant remark made by someone close to you. Again, corrective action of some kind, even if it's just a matter of 'clarifying the situation' can be taken and the stress will vanish once a solution is found. Unfortunately, on the whole, psychological problems are not as easy to correct as physical ones, and what is known as chronic stress can occur. Usually this is brought about by a sustained series of shocks or unpleasant events, or by remorseless psychological pressures being placed upon us. Stress of this kind is not easily removed, and apart from its deeply debilitating effect on the sufferer's mood and personality, the persistent physiological and emotional changes which go hand in hand with it tend to build up and induce even longer-term side effects.

Life here on Earth is full of discrepancies. We are endlessly trying to rise to impossible challenges. We strive continuously to see logic in nonsense. This is a bizarre place where the oddest people of all are the ones who consider themselves to be perfectly sane. Little wonder we sometimes feel as though we're fighting a losing battle. Even so, it is still possible to manipulate a flawed system to your advantage. Do what you know will work, and don't worry about why it works or whether or not it really ought to work! Even though you are bound to make an error every so often, they are mistakes you will learn from and ultimately profit from. Have faith in all you are doing, even if, so far, not much of it seems to be working. If you trust you heart you simply have to end up with what you need. We are surrounded by shining examples of what can be accomplished with dedication. You want your share of the spoils. You can have most of it. But not immediately!

People are perversely attracted to the complicated, the difficult and the stressful. We like the sound of easy options; but only if we can tell, instinctively, that they are not really as easy as they seem. If shown a genuine, simple way to make things work, we feel suspicious. If told about a problem of some kind, we walk towards it with open arms, ready to accept what must be a punishment we deserve. You can now get all steamed up about something irritating. You can get into it, add to it and turn it into something big. Or you can decide to leave it alone. This does not amount to giving up or running away. It simply represents a wiser approach.

Stress is like quicksand. Once you fall into it, you'll find it hard to pull yourself out again. The more you struggle and try to extricate yourself, the deeper you will sink. How can you avoid such a fate? Begin by checking that you are not already stuck. Is there a grudge you can't stop nursing, a resentment you can't ignore, a fear you feel intimidated by, a complaint you are determined to make? Disentangle yourself from negative emotion. Resist the urge to get further into something you need to let go of. Then, only the right things will happen from that moment on.

What is stressful for one person may not necessarily be so for another, and in the long run it is a matter of how well one is able to control the pressures and challenges that life presents. Most people gradually learn what their own limitations are and manage to avoid exceedingly stressful situations. Others seem to thrive on stress, though what they actually thrive on is the solving of problems which to other people would appear stressful.

Why is it that sometimes the easiest things seem to be daunting? Why do we end up struggling with problems we ought to sweep aside? Various people have various theories about this. Some think the universe deliberately clouds our judgement, or puts us in difficult situations in order to test us. Maybe that's the case, maybe not. Even so, every now and then, we make a significant breakthrough. We see the big picture, what needs to be done, and how to do it. When we gain such clarity, it helps us resolve many issues and fulfil many desires.

Life doesn't always have to be complicated, stressful or troublesome. But it does have to be this way from time to time. If there were never any problems, we would have no misery to compare our joy to. How then would we appreciate happiness? The ratio, though, needs to be right. Not too much pain for too little gain. Right thinking will rectify the imbalance. But it will only stay right once you understand what made it go wrong in the first place. Look back deeply enough and you'll gain an insight that will steer you towards a brighter future.

There are times when we should be thankful for our problems. Our difficulties can be helpful in ways we do not appreciate at the time. A lack of resources may be an irritation while you are enduring it, but, when you look back and realise how much time and effort you might have wasted on a wild notion, had you only been able to, you'll probably be relieved that your resources were restricted. Even when you do manage to free yourself from a limitation, this doesn't mean that you should go wild! There's usually a good reason why some things are not as easy to get as you would like them to be!

Now and then, the more difficult or even traumatic events in our life can be more beneficial to us than the undemanding and satisfying ones. They can galvanise us into action and cause us to re-evaluate our true priorities. You may not be sure yet whether what you feel is false bravado or a genuine new sense of determination. Who knows what tomorrow will bring? Coming events may give you good reason to be grateful for all those earlier unpleasant experiences. Be wise enough to see that problems are not always a bad thing. And expect stress, followed by success.

Sometimes, if you want to stop things from going wrong, you have to assert that you don't care if they do go wrong. You can be too nervous. You can be too apprehensive. If you dwell on something, or harbour feelings of foreboding about it, you can often end up creating the very problem you are most keen to avoid. Take a long look at your situation. How concerned should you be? See the difference between a real danger and a perceived one. When you do, you will have reached a moment of revelation and realisation. You'll gain an insight that could affect the rest of your life. Now, what are you taking too seriously? It's time to cure an unfounded fear.

How can you be sure what the truth about your situation really is? What if you are merely reflecting your biased perspective on a multifaceted matter? Some truths are relative, and not everything in this world is as straightforward as it seems. All I am trying to suggest is that most things can be viewed from different angles, and how you see them can often depend upon where you are standing at the time. The front of something can often appear far more attractive than the back; take a horse, for example. Positive processes can often have stressful side effects. We always have a choice about which end of a situation we focus on. When you're up against a seemingly insurmountable obstacle or a source of stress, you just need to find a way to see the other side of it.

It is possible to suffer from stress and not know it. And what's more, this is often the most damaging and upsetting manifestation of the problem. Not all the forces that throw us into a state of physiological or psychological alert are immediately recognizable to us. If you are going to live in the real world, you cannot hope to eliminate stress totally. The only alternative would be to lead a reclusive existence in which you never put yourself in any kind of uncomfortable or unnerving situation. Under such circumstances life might be safe, but very dull. Your aim must not be to avoid stressful situations altogether, but rather to do everything that you can to find solutions to them when they arise and avoid getting yourself into chronic conditions which produce unpleasant physical and psychological side effects. This may not be as difficult as it sounds. Often it is a matter of merely identifying the stressful situation; it is amazing how many people cannot grasp this simple fact. Sometimes a friend or a loved one, or even an impartial observer can help in pointing out the origin of a conflict that is putting you under prolonged stress.

Life has its ups and downs; there's no escaping that reality. Nothing we say or do will alter that fact; we simply have to acknowledge it. But we can decide to accept and adapt to the circumstances that we find ourselves facing. When we do, the blues are not so blue. The downs are not so deep and they do not last so long. What really creates stress is the desire to avoid the inevitable. Embrace it instead. Try to be accepting; even of what you feel you simply cannot accept. You may think something is inevitable, but it is not. You will only gain the power to change it once you are no longer afraid or resentful of it.

You may feel as though you have been through more than you can stand. You have been put to the test and led to the end of your tether. The stress is beginning to become unbearable. You feel that you have so little to spare that the tiniest drain on your resources is going to seem like an enormous burden. Try to shrug off that sense of exhaustion and exasperation. I know this is easier said than done. You probably think you'll need a miracle to accomplish this. If so, how many miracles? Just the one. How big a miracle does it need to be? Not very big at all, really. In fact, you are not looking for a miracle. You just need a succession of serendipitous circumstances to come your way. Unbelievable things can often turn out to be entirely credible. Seemingly impossible challenges can appear less daunting. So much so that you simply take them in your stride. You have the wherewithal to fulfil your deepest desires. It is not a miracle you need. It is just a belief in your own ability.

Sometimes, we forget how strong we are. We let our concerns overshadow everything else, even though there's nothing to be concerned about. We hark back to old problems and forget that we have long since learnt how to deal with them. We see ourselves as vulnerable children instead of mature adults. We think we need protection when, actually, we are perfectly capable of protecting ourselves. The truth is, you face nothing that you can't take in your stride.

# CHAPTER 18
# YOU ARE WHAT YOU THINK

The Law of Attraction (Cause and Effect) states that you are capable of attracting into your life the people, circumstances, opportunities, ideas and knowledge you need to attain your desires. When you think positive, encouraging, optimistic and pleasant thoughts, you create an energy that draws these favourable conditions towards you. If you keep your thoughts firmly focused on what you want, and avoid thinking about what you don't want, you will ultimately attract whatever you need to succeed.

Successful people are those who think more positively and productively than their unsuccessful counterparts. They habitually think thoughts of abundance, happiness and success and don't allow any contradictory thoughts to enter their minds. Their foremost thoughts are of wealth, success and growth.

You physically, psychologically and emotionally advance towards whatever image you fix in your mind, whether it is in your best interest or not. For as long as you hold that image, you will be drawn towards it. Your self-image controls your overall demeanour and performance. Unless you change the image you have of yourself, you will continue to get the same results.

The life you're leading now is a reflection of your predominant thoughts. Since you attract into your life what you continually think about, it isn't hard to see what your overriding thoughts have been on every aspect of your life; because whatever you have experienced up until now will be the result of those thoughts.

Anything that your conscious mind believes is true will also be regarded as true by your subconscious, whatever it may be. Your subconscious is hugely influenced by the continual thinking of your conscious mind. For this reason, you must steer clear of any negative or damaging thoughts, because once they are embraced by your conscious mind, your subconscious will also accept them and do its utmost to bring them to fruition. As you can see, the conscious mind acts as a lookout. It is there to shield your subconscious mind from incorrect or mistaken assumptions.

You need to bear in mind that, if you want to change your circumstances, you must do it from the inside out, because the outside-in approach doesn't work! The practical solution to hardship, lack, poverty and deprivation is to change your thoughts of limitation and failure to thoughts of abundance and success. When your habitual thinking is positive, pleasant and constructive, you can form new, beneficial and creative habits that will be to your long-term advantage.

You begin the process of changing the way you think by altering your self-image. You must develop a clear-cut, distinct, unique, confident, inspiring and good-natured attitude, consistent with the most positive image you have of yourself. You develop an ideal self-image by visualizing yourself performing to the highest standards in everything you undertake. If you believe that you are an outstanding person, brimming with talent, aptitude and expertise, and that you're destined to achieve great things, these fundamental beliefs will drive you to set goals, work productively, improve your prospects, be more considerate, cope with setbacks, and ultimately achieve your goals.

Everyone has a subconscious image of the type of house they should be living in, the car they should be driving, the kind of people they should socialize with, etc. This mental image reflects your comfort zone, which is where you feel you belong. Any time you find yourself straying from this image, anxiety and stress will follow. That little voice inside your head will tell you to "get back to where you belong," compelling you to return to more familiar surroundings, where you subconsciously feel more at ease. If you succumb to this little voice, changing your life will become a long-drawn-out process.

Whatever you're feeling about yourself right now is being expressed in every facet of your life. Your strength, temperament, health, financial situation, friends and social status are a precise indication of the way you view yourself. This is what you are impressing into your subconscious mind, and what you're experiencing throughout each day of your life. Whatever you impress on your subconscious mind, you will also encounter as situations, experiences and events. For this reason you must carefully monitor every thought, idea and concept that enters your conscious mind.

As a result of being criticized and undermined when we were children, we tend to be more cautious, inhibited and uncertain when we become adults. We would rather play it safe than take any risks, for fear of ridicule. We quit before we've even started. We may desperately want to try something new, but we are afraid of failure and disappointment. But mostly we are afraid of incurring the disapproval or contempt of those around us.

For many people, the fear of failure and rejection is their overriding concern. They want to accomplish something that will improve their current situation; but they are afraid that if they fail, they will be leaving themselves open to criticism. They crave approval and acceptance over achievement and abundance. They constantly feel the need to please others, even if this is to the detriment of themselves.

What can't you do? What can't you have? Why not? What makes you so sure? If you put up protective barriers against an imaginary foe, you are limiting yourself unnecessarily. Don't you know how powerful you are and how influential you can be? You may be presuming that someone is in a position to harm you, when, in fact, they pose no threat to you whatsoever; thus, you are wasting valuable energy on a needless defence plan. Life on planet Earth is not always simple and clear-cut. You need clarity. That's not such a tall order. Begin simply by looking for comfort and reassurance. You will find that more easily than you expect. Once you start to feel less worried, you will see exactly what you are supposed to do to make things just the way they are supposed to be. Have more faith in yourself and be less intimidated by a problem. Remember, the best is yet to come and the journey from here to there starts now!

Instead of constantly dwelling on what you fear or dread, you should be embracing what you desire. This makes perfect sense. Never judge yourself by your past performances. Recognise that you are a self-made person and that your success or failure is entirely in your hands.

Sometimes, we can put ourselves through unnecessary misery by projecting fears into the future. Instead of taking a situation moment by moment at face value, we read endless levels of meaning into it. We prejudge and dread a future that has yet to arrive, and then wonder why we feel so hemmed in. Don't sit worrying about something that hasn't happened; and may never happen. The harder you try to plan for every eventuality, the harder you will make it for a stroke of sudden luck to enter into your life. Because magic can, and will, flow into your life as soon as you create a little room for it.

If everyone in the world has a mental filing cabinet, it must be full of folders. Suppose there's one labelled 'Worthless', and another marked 'Worthwhile'. They adjoin one another for alphabetic purposes. Yet, sadly, this means that when hurriedly tidying up the office of the mind, we can sometimes, inadvertently, mix up the data in those two crucial sections. Just such a subconscious switch may have occurred in your life. As soon as you spot this, you must rectify it immediately. As a result, you will notice a marked improvement in your circumstances. Once you see what you've overlooked, clarity and understanding will follow.

As I stated earlier, you physically, emotionally and psychologically move towards whatever you believe and envisage. Your beliefs and opinions about yourself determine everything you do and everything that happens to you. Therefore, it is important to control your thoughts. You must visualize your desired outcome. What exactly do you want? If you cannot picture it or describe it, you cannot achieve it.

People with positive self-images motivate themselves to excel in their chosen field. They set high standards for themselves and continually strive to meet these goals. If they suffer setbacks or disappointments along the way, they take them in their stride; because they know they will succeed in the end. They stubbornly persist until they accomplish their objective, even if the odds are stacked against them. This is the mark of a true winner.

Fulfilling your true potential requires a great deal of determination and self-belief. You must be prepared to step outside of your comfort zone. But, if you truly believe in yourself, you will be willing to do this. If you desire success so strongly that it almost becomes an obsession, you will have no difficulty motivating yourself to do whatever is needed to attain it. But you must truly want success; not as a wish, or a longing, but as a consuming passion.

A famous golfer once remarked, "It's a strange thing, but the more I practise, the luckier I seem to get." Hard work, to some extent at least, creates good fortune. Effort invariably leads to reward. It is, though, true that a small amount of effort can sometimes bring a very big reward, and a large amount won't necessarily bring results in the same proportion. That, of course, is because there's more than one ingredient in the recipe of success.

Successful people recognise that simply hoping and longing for success will not bring you closer to your goal. But desiring success so strongly and intensely that it dominates your waking hours and compels you to find ways and means to achieve it, will set in motion a process of transformation that can only have a positive outcome.

The best things in life require imagination, effort, faith and commitment. How difficult is it to attain these? Extremely difficult if you are not inspired. Quite the opposite if you have passion, enthusiasm, vision and understanding. So, if you are inspired, what can you do with all these qualities? What can you create? What can you convert them into? Anything you like, or nothing if you prefer. They are not a means to an end. They are an end in themselves. You need to reach for what inspires you; then what you need, you will get.

# CHAPTER 19
# YOUR ULTIMATE GOAL

The call of destiny isn't a fanfare or a clarion call. Instead it is a tantalizing vision, an inexplicable impulse, a nudge from within. It is also a magnetic pull towards an idea or a course of action. Have you experienced any such sensation? Are you heeding or resisting it? Change can be scary, but this call is definitely inviting you to make a wise choice and a bold move. Allow yourself to respond to it. A courageous choice on your part now could improve everything.

If you can't rely on your instincts, what can you rely on? For, whether you're aware of it or not, deep down inside there is a part of you that knows what's best for you and knows, too, what's ill-judged. You may choose to ignore it, but that doesn't mean it isn't there. All you need to do is be open and receptive to this guidance and you will be steered in the right direction.

There is a benevolent force watching over you. Listen out for hints and suggestions that may not be immediately obvious. Someone, somewhere is whispering. This person is not necessarily trying to be secretive; it's just that they don't feel the need to shout. They are just trying to gently guide you. If you listen, you will be taken away from a source of stress and given a new reason to be hopeful. You may be led in a number of ways, from a helpful chain of events to a remarkable coincidence, or even the direct intervention of someone who has your best interests at heart. So, be sensitive now and you could learn something to your advantage.

You are entitled to your dream. You are also entitled to the chance to try to make it come true. You may not want to do this. You may decide that your dream is providing you with a very comfortable escape mechanism. Were it to become a reality, it might also become a liability. But that is a choice for you to make. And it should be made through discrimination, not defeatism. Don't be too scared to take the opportunity to pursue your dream. Err on the side of caution, not on the side of pessimism. Give it all you've got and it will give you, in return, a sense of lasting reassurance.

Determine in advance that you are never going to give up until you have achieved your goal. The major ingredients of persistence are the strength of your determination and the intensity of your desire. Whenever willpower and desire join forces, they make an irresistible combination. Many people quit at the first obstacle or misfortune they encounter. But the determined ones carry on despite all the setbacks. If you lack persistence you are more likely to fail in your objective. Whether you succeed or not will depend upon the strength of your desire. By making a conscious decision never to give up, you are giving yourself a psychological advantage. So, whenever problems occur, you will be ready and prepared for any eventuality. If you constantly focus on your ultimate goal with desire and determination, from that moment on, you will not be hindered by a lack of persistence.

Many people are reluctant to take chances because they're afraid of the criticism they will receive if they fail. In many cases their fear of criticism is greater than their appetite for success. They avoid setting high standards for themselves because they are concerned about how their friends and relatives will judge them if they fail. So they refuse to pursue their goal for fear of being laughed at and ridiculed.

Taking charge of your own destiny can be a lonely course of action, and sometimes it may feel as though everyone is against you; but the only person you should be concerned about is yourself.

Other people's opinions are irrelevant and inconsequential. Others will have opinions and beliefs that are different from yours, and when they see you living your life according to your beliefs, they'll feel frightened and insecure. They are fearful because, as they see it, if you are right, they must be wrong. That's a bitter pill for them to swallow. Insecure people will always feel threatened by anyone who opposes their principal beliefs.

Some people think they have the definitive answers to all our questions. But, have you ever noticed how they never, under any circumstances, utter those three magic words "I don't know". But sometimes, of course, they don't know. They really don't. And then, because they dare not admit as much, they tend to bluff or assume. You suspect you know what's right, but you are being told otherwise by someone who seems to have more authority than you do. Don't allow yourself to assume that they know all the answers.

The world seems to be full of people who are absolutely brimming with self-confidence, self-assurance and self-importance. They know what they think, they know what they believe, they know (or reckon they know) who they are and what their purpose in life is. Indeed, about the only thing they don't seem to know is how tedious and tiresome they are, or how ill-informed. You may not always be so sure of yourself. That's an advantage, not a drawback. It means you often ask the right questions. It also means that when you feel very strongly about something, you are probably right.

The most important principal belief you can embrace is that you are a decent, honest and hard-working person who is destined to be successful and happy. You should also believe that every difficulty is only a temporary setback that you will ultimately overcome, and that you will accomplish any goal you set for yourself. When you take these fundamental beliefs on board, your success will be virtually guaranteed. If you have high self-esteem, you will also have a high opinion of yourself; and the higher the opinion you have of yourself, the more decisive, positive and courageous you will be. You will be energized and better able to focus your attention on where you want to go and what you want to achieve. You will feel strong and confident, and able to do the very best of which you are capable.

Self improvement is one of the best ways to save time. The more proficient and confident you are in your work, the more you relish the job in hand. You will become enthusiastic and passionate about achieving your goal, and because of this you will get a lot more done in a shorter period of time. This is true; when you know that you can do something well, you naturally tend to get the job done better and faster. Never allow a perceived inability or weakness to discourage you or hold you back. All skills are attainable. If others have managed to learn them, then you can too. Set about learning whatever skills are necessary for you to become more productive and effective. Continually learning new skills will help you feel strong, confident and enthusiastic about what you do; and people around you will pick up on those feelings. Enthusiasm is contagious. If you are passionate about your work, others will be carried along by the strength of your conviction.

Everything you create in life begins with a single thought. The greater the desire you have to be successful, the more you will accomplish. Successful people constantly dream big dreams; they imagine that they have no limitations holding them back from achieving whatever they desire. Therefore, you must visualize your goals repeatedly, intently and vividly; this will help galvanize, energize and incentivize you. You will obtain better results if you visualize your desires just before you go to sleep, when you are entering into a drowsy state, or just after you wake up; because your conscious, reasoning mind is less resistant when in a sleepy state.

For you to fulfil your desires, you must free yourself from any limiting beliefs. You need to eradicate any negative and adverse thoughts that are hampering your chances of success. Only by doing this will you discover how to unearth, develop and reveal the abilities, skills and knowledge that you possess. What unique talents do you have? What are you especially good at? What do you enjoy doing? Take some time to think about what specialized skills you have that you can use to your advantage. These will invariably be the tasks in which you excel, and that give you the most satisfaction.

Never allow yourself to be daunted by the size of the task that lies ahead of you. The most effective way to avoid becoming overwhelmed is to do one task at a time. No matter how big, complicated or intimidating the job in front of you may seem to be, just concentrate on doing one vital task, and see it through to completion. Just by developing the habit of starting and completing one assignment, and then moving onto the next and so on, you will soon realise that you can accomplish more than you thought was possible.

If you don't ever start, you can't ever finish. If you don't ever finish, you can't ever start again. Endings and beginnings are scary. The longer we postpone them, the less challenge we feel we have to contend with. Are you not sure how much of yourself to give to your current opportunity? What if it has an outcome that is even more challenging? That's a risk you have to take. Something within you is beckoning you like a finger of fate. Follow it and follow your heart too, for both forces will guide you in the right direction, along the path that leads to a positive change.

To be successful you must continually push yourself to perform at the highest level. You should continually strive to better yourself because there's always room for improvement; always try to go that little bit further, or do more than is necessary or expected. Set deadlines for yourself and make sure you always meet them. By exerting this sort of pressure on yourself, you achieve more and you complete your tasks quicker than you were previously able to. This in turn builds up your confidence, and you feel more motivated and enthused about tackling your workload. You quickly develop the habit of completing all your vital tasks, which makes you a far more efficient performer.

When you suffer the inevitable setbacks and difficulties that occur from time to time, never let them dishearten you; always try your best to remain optimistic. Try to find something good or advantageous to salvage from a difficult situation. If you look hard enough, you can usually find something useful to learn from most bad experiences. Always look at ways in which you can solve your problems. Instead of moaning and whining when things go wrong, devote your time and energy into the valuable task of solving the problem. You won't achieve anything by wasting time complaining about it.

Constantly think about how you're going to achieve your goals, and what you hope to accomplish in the future. Always look at the road ahead, and not in the rear-view mirror. Keep yourself focused on moving forward towards a better future; and on what you must do to improve your life. This will have the effect of making you feel much more positive and give you the incentive you need to get started on your vital tasks. It will also make you more determined to keep on going, through the good times, and the bad.

Continually look for ways in which you can save yourself time. Plan your day ahead by choosing each individual task that needs to be done, and the amount of time you wish to spend on it. Be sure to devote your time only to important tasks; the ones that will have the most substantive long-term effects. Spend your time wisely. Plan and prepare all your jobs in advance, and then launch yourself quickly into them. You should have a clear idea of what your goals and objectives are for each day; and you must work tirelessly to complete them. If you work steadily and continuously in this manner, you'll be amazed at the amount of work you get through. What separates a truly professional person from an average one is the time that he takes to prepare. The person who isn't entirely serious often attempts to struggle through with a minimum amount of preparation; whereas the committed person will meticulously plan each day ahead. To put it clearly, concisely and succinctly: 'IF YOU FAIL TO PREPARE, YOU PREPARE TO FAIL'.

An effective method you can employ to deal with huge tasks is to spend a specific amount of time each day on them. This can be as small a time period as you feel comfortable with, maybe as little as a few minutes. You decide how much time you spend on each task; and when you feel as though you've had enough, you simply stop and do something else. You'll find this technique very useful, especially when you're faced with a task that you previously would have considered overwhelming.

Your skill in prioritising your tasks in order of importance and then completing them tenaciously and accurately is the crucial ingredient needed to ensure your success. The key to high productivity lies in your ability to determine which vital tasks need to be taken on, and in what order; along with your dogged determination that you will not stop until each task is completed. Once you've mastered this simple technique, you'll be amazed at the effect it has on you. It increases your enthusiasm and motivation. You feel more energetic, and you gain a great deal of satisfaction in seeing your workload gradually decreasing. Working non-stop on one task at a time means you get more done in less time. You become more resolute in your self-belief, and you feel more confident and happy as you see yourself develop into someone who is far more competent and productive.

As you become more disciplined, efficient and self-assured, you will be compelled to work to the maximum of your ability on the tasks that are most crucial to your success. This will inevitably guarantee that you do become successful. And the more successful you become, the busier you will become. And the busier you become, the bigger your workload will be. This is when you'll probably find that there is never enough time to complete all your tasks. When faced with this situation, you must always remember that there is never enough time to get everything done, but there is always time to get the important things done. You usually find out the hard way how much you can do; and you determine this by trying to do too much. Only by stretching yourself to your absolute limits can you discover what your limitations are. But the upside of this is, you also discover what you are capable of achieving. So, for you to be totally successful, you must work to the very limits of your ability. But, if you truly love what you're doing this will be less of a challenge.

Whatever we do the most we get good at. If we practise the piano every day, we become good pianists. If we regularly stand on one leg, we develop good balance. And if we frequently become irritable and anxious? Well, that's the point. Habits are hard to break. Somewhere in your life now there's a pattern that is being repeated too often. You deserve better. And you can have better too. All you have to do is recognise that it is time to start doing less of one thing, and more of another!

Persistence is an absolute necessity if you are to succeed in achieving your goal; it is an invaluable asset to have. If you are able to keep going, even when faced with the inevitable and unavoidable setbacks that you are bound to encounter from time to time, this will prove that you have the right temperament to succeed. Your success will be guaranteed if you unrelentingly pursue your goals with dogged determination and an unshakeable resolve never to give up. Constantly affirm the following: 'FAILURE ISN'T AN OPTION'.

You always behave in a manner that's in keeping with your dominant beliefs, especially your beliefs about yourself. As a consequence, you naturally reject any information you consider to be of no value to you, or which threatens your principal beliefs. Any information that isn't deemed useful to you will be rejected offhand and not allowed to get through, much like a spam filter on your e-mail.

Whatever beliefs you have today are the result of the messages you received in early childhood. The beliefs that you adopt when you are young can affect you for the rest of your life. For instance, let's imagine that when you were nine years old a teacher called you 'stupid'. That statement enters your subconscious mind and remains there. Your subconscious mind believes all the information it receives is true; unlike your conscious mind, it does not reason things out.

It simply accepts whatever information you give it. So, from that moment on, your subconscious mind considers it to be a statement of fact that you are stupid. Each time you recall the incident it gets embedded deeper into your subconscious, thus reinforcing your mistaken belief, which is "I am stupid". The teacher's thoughtless statement soon becomes a dominant belief, whereas in reality it was simply a casual observation. As you grow up, you continue to believe that you are stupid. Over the years this becomes an entrenched, deep-rooted belief. That being so, you have allowed one careless, thoughtless remark to alter the entire course of your life, because once you allow this type of viewpoint to dominate your thinking, you will unconsciously act in accordance with this belief; thereby living a self-fulfilling prophecy. As is often the case, the teacher is oblivious to the impact his comment has had on you and how it has affected you throughout your life. Many people's lives have been ruined by the thoughtless and insensitive remarks or actions of others. Don't allow yourself to become one of these needless victims.

Never judge people or situations until you have gathered enough information to make an informed opinion. Crucially, you must not judge, criticize or blame yourself for not living up to the expectations of yourself or others. Your most firmly established beliefs about yourself and your capabilities may be mistaken.

The most damaging beliefs are self-limiting beliefs. These occur when you consider yourself to be inferior in some areas, or think you are less able or competent than others. As a result, you constantly undervalue and underestimate your capabilities and end up settling for less than you deserve. These self-limiting beliefs hinder your chances of success. They create uncertainty, indecision and insecurity. They immobilize you and leave you feeling anxious and self-conscious. You are left feeling apprehensive and unsure if you are able or willing to take the vital move forward. For you to develop and advance your life, you must constantly confront and question your self-limiting beliefs. This means disregarding any notion or suggestion that you are inferior to others. Focus your mind on the basic premise that you are a worthy and competent person who is capable of achieving anything you set your mind to.

Your unlimited potential lies in your ability to control your thoughts. An indecisive, constrained mind will result in weakness, disappointment and frustration, whereas a resolute, inventive mind will enjoy success, wealth and happiness. Therefore, you must be decisive about what you want to achieve and never allow anyone or anything to come between what you believe and what you want. Deep down inside, you know what you really want, and if you listen to your inner voice, you will be guided towards it. Your conscious mind may occasionally fail you, but your intuition won't.

Your instincts are the key to self-empowerment. If we can only understand what's going on inside us, we can be clearer about what we want. This could make it much easier for us to fulfil our true potential. We begin to realise how a hope we once dismissed as impractical could prove feasible. This thought is inspiring, but also intimidating. That's good! Your goals should both excite and frighten you.

You have exceptional powers and abilities. Your insights and sensitivities are valuable gifts which, if used wisely, can be put to a constructive purpose. Don't doubt this just because you recognise that you are not infallible. Nobody in this world gets exactly what they want whenever they want it. Those of us who wish to be truly wise are more inclined to accept guidance from higher forces, even if this conflicts with our own opinion about what should be happening. It is simply a matter of standing back and being clever. Everything you are looking for is within you. Somewhere, deep in the very heart of your mind, your soul, your spirit, is the instinctive answer to a key question. You just need to trust that.

# ABOUT THE AUTHOR

Chris Hopkins' early working life consisted of various run-of-the-mill office jobs: office junior, filing clerk, vdu operator, etc. Unchallenging and undemanding jobs that never tested him intellectually or emotionally. He felt trapped by his circumstances and frustrated that he wasn't fulfilling his true potential. It wasn't until he was in his mid thirties that he decided to try and improve his situation. He embarked upon a change of career; he went into sales. He soon discovered that he had a natural flair for this type of work and it wasn't long before he began to work his way to the top. With the experience he gained he went on to run his own home-based sales company and write a book titled "150+ WAYS TO WIN OVER CUSTOMERS AND MAKE THAT SALE". He now works as a freelance copywriter, writing promotional material for both large and small companies.